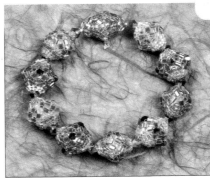

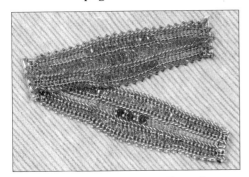

The Passion of Beading with Delicas

History of Delica Beads

The popularity of Delica Beads® by MIYUKI for stunning jewelry and bead bags has become widespread. It began with the founding of a Japanese bead company in the 1930s. With a small variety of initial bead types, MIYUKI first produced only transparent and opaque small beads.

While MIYUKI worked toward improvements in quality, beaded bags and beaded dresses grew in demand. Around 1960, Japan's Empress Michiko used a bead embroidery bag that triggered a wave of popularity. Beads of higher quality with an increase in the number of colors were produced. MIYUKI also developed plating technology for silver lined beads.

Regarding the birth of Delica beads, customers inquired about the feasibility of producing beads which were suitable for weaving in terms of shape. Beaders wanted small, delicate and elegant beads for bead bags like the ones cherished by noblewomen in Europe in the 19th century.

With an eye toward this, MIYUKI developed beads suitable in shape... cylindrical beads which are uniform in shape with large holes (allowing several strings to pass through).

The most difficult part in manufacturing these beads was cutting. Since the thickness of the glass is thin, glass is easily broken and it becomes very hard to cut glass tubes. As a result of continuous trial and error, it became feasible to make innovative beads which are uniform in shape by developing a special cutting machine and devising a method of heating to cut pieces evenly. MIYUKI named these elegant and exquisite beads "Delica Beads." The name was adopted from the word delicacy in English.

Delica bead weaving evoked enthusiasm in Japan and in the U.S. MIYUKI began to teach "Delica bead weaving" and establish schools to popularize it. They educated beaders, trained teachers, and established the "Delica Bead Loom Association" in Japan. The Association is in its 23rd year with members totaling 4,500 people and 500 teachers.

Looking back, the progress of the development of Delica beads and the opening of the MIYUKI bead factory have led to increased bead enthusiasts.

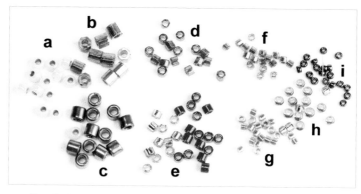

Beads from left to right:

(a) Miyuki size 8/0 seed bead, #198, copper-lined satin;

(b) Delica size 8/0 cut, DBL89C, luster black-lined amber;

(c) Delica size 8/0 plain, DBL29, metallic purple/gold iris;

(d) Delica size 10/0 cut, DBM103C, dusty rose with gold luster;

(e) Delica size 10/0, DBM146, silver-lined light amethyst transparent; DBM105, light luster transparent crimson;

(f) Delica size 11/0 cut, DB89C, luster black-lined amber;

(g) Delica size 11/0, DB58, luster blue-lined clear;

(h) Miyuki size 11/0 seed bead, #12, silver-lined light amethyst transparent;

(i) Miyuki size 15/0 seed bead, #455, black iris AB.

	Bead	size	type	width in mm	length in mm
●	Delica	8/0	cut	3.0	3.0
●	Delica	8/0	plain	3.0	3.0
●	Round	8/0		3.0	2.0
●	Delica	10/0	cut	2.2	1.7
●	Delica	10/0	plain	2.2	1.7
●	Round	11/0		2.0	1.4
●	Delica	11/0	cut	1.6	1.4
●	Delica	11/0	plain	1.6	1.4
●	Round	15/0		1.5	1.0

Needles

The large holes in all Delica sizes make it possible to work many of these projects with size 10 beading needles.

However, you will have to use size 12 or 13 needles for projects that incorporate seed beads or have many thread passes.

MIYUKI

Delica beads, also known generically as Japanese cylinder beads, are cylindrical in shape and very regular. They were invented by Mr. Masayoshi Katsuoka, president of Miyuki Company, in the early 1980s, and the original size, 11/0, arrived in the United States in 1987. Size 8/0 followed in the mid-1990s. And Miyuki developed the new size 10/0 within the last 2-3 years.

All three sizes come in both the original plain cylinder and the hexagonal or "cut" shape. You will find very few irregular beads in packages of size 10 and 11 plain Delicas. Size 8/0 Delicas evince slightly more irregularity; and while cuts have been fire polished to produce smooth edges, a few may have sharp ends, so choose them with care.

In fact, to get the best results, you should always select Delicas and other kinds of beads carefully; even in the most regular of brands there will always be slight size and length variations in a package.

Seed beads are measured across the width of their hole (the diameter) to determine size. The length of the hole is irrelevant to their size; although it has a major impact on what kinds of beads can be used together. Using different length beads together, however, can create remarkable texture.

The type of finish applied to the bead may also affect its size slightly. Even glass type has an effect on size – black beads of any type are almost always a bit smaller than other colors of the same type, for example.

In the photo, beads a, b, and c at left are all size 8/0. Notice the two a and b beads that are aligned hole to hole in the photo. While their width is almost identical, the difference in their length is dramatic. Size 8/0 round seed beads (a) average about 2.9mm in width but are about 2mm in length. Cut (b) and plain (c) size 8/0 Delicas average 2.9 to 3.05mm in width but are almost 1mm longer than round size 8/0s.

Beads d & e are size 10/0 Delicas; the d beads are cuts & the e beads are plain. Cut size 10/0 Delicas average 2.05mm in width & 1.65mm in length. Plain size 10/0 Delicas are a hair narrower & longer. Size 10/0 Delicas are closest in size to size 11/0 round Japanese seed beads (h), which average 2.15mm in width but are about 0.3mm shorter. The similarity in size of 10/0 Delicas & 11/0 Miyuki seeds makes them suitable to be used together.

Size 11/0 Delicas (f cuts & g) are markedly smaller than size 11/0 seed beads (h) but only a little larger than size 15/0 seed beads (i), revealed by the adjacent f & i beads lying on their sides. Delica size 11/0 beads (f & g) average 1.7mm in width & 1.4mm in length. Size 15/0 round seed beads (i) vary a lot in any given package but average 1.6mm in width & 1mm in length.

Threads

You should, of course, use your favorite needles and threads. Many beaders swear by the strength of Fireline, but I haven't used it since a piece I'd woven on Fireline came apart in a million pieces. I was a Nymo beader until very recently Kobayashi introduced new nylon filament thread offered in slightly different palettes. Kobayashi's new thread is K-O. The weight is similar to Nymo B, but the thread has a slick coating that causes it to resist fraying without needing any type of thread conditioner (beeswax or Thread Heaven). It also seems to be comparable in strength to Nymo D.

K-O has recently produced a D weight that seems much stronger than Nymo D.

K-O and Nymo both need to be prestretched before you begin to weave. K-O is very stretchy, so prestretching will prevent your beadwork from becoming loose over time. It also uncoils the thread, which helps minimize tangling. As with any thread, you should thread the needle with the end that comes off the spool first so you are sewing with the thread's grain to minimize fraying.

If you are using beads with sharp edges, such as crystals or some cuts, you may prefer to use Fireline or Power Pro (BeadCats sells a generic version of the latter at a much reduced price). I used K-O for all the projects in this book.

Scissors and Glue

My favorite beading scissors are high-quality, Solingen steel manicure scissors. They're very sharp, sturdy, and come to a tiny point. Good-quality "stork" embroidery scissors also work well. When cutting off thread tails, use a trick Virginia Blakelock teaches and pull on the thread as you cut it. This stretches it slightly so the end hides inside the last bead.

Never cut a thread immediately after a knot; pass it through a few beads before cutting, or the knot will come untied.

If you use clear nail polish as glue for your knots, apply a drop from the tip of your beading needle directly on the knot (another Virginia Blakelock trick). Never use the nail polish brush; the solvent could damage bead color or finish. I recommend G-S Hypo Cement for knots at the end of pearl strands.

Basic Knots

Surgeon's Knot

The surgeon's knot starts like a square knot.

1. Cross the left-hand end on top of the right-hand end, wrap it behind the right-hand cord, and bring it back to the front (lower blue line).

The right-hand tail (red) now points left and the left-hand tail points right.

2. Bend the right-hand tail (red) back toward the right and the left-hand tail back toward the left (middle of knot).

3. Cross the tail that's currently on the right (blue), over the tail coming from the left (red).

4. Wrap it behind that tail and pull it through the opening between the step 1 cross and the step 3 cross (this is a square knot).

5. To turn it into a surgeon's knot wrap behind, under, and through to the front again.

The result is that the top of the knot curves partway down the sides of the first cross, which makes it more stable and unlikely to twist out of the square when you tighten it.

6. Pull the tails in the directions they are pointing to tighten the knot.

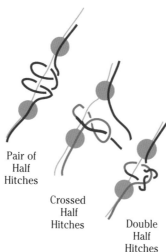

Pair of Half Hitches

Crossed Half Hitches

Double Half Hitches

Half-Hitch Knot

1. For a plain half hitch, bring the needle through a bead. Then sew under the thread between this bead and the next bead. Tighten until a small loop remains.

2. Pass the needle through the loop, going over the thread you previously sewed under (lower loop in pair of half hitches).

3. Repeat the process for a paired half hitch, which is more secure than a single half hitch.

4. For a crossed half hitch, repeat step 1 of the plain half hitch. Give the starting loop a half twist so its sides cross (red loop on right), then sew through it. Tighten carefully so it doesn't lock too soon.

5. Start a double half hitch like a plain half hitch but sew through the loop twice. This knot is prone to tightening prematurely.

Crimping

You can press a crimp flat with chain-nose pliers, but crimping pliers fold the crimp so it is less visible and slightly more secure. The jaws of crimping pliers have two stations. The one closer to the handles looks like a crescent moon, and the one at the end of the pliers is oval.

1. Separate the wires in the crimp with one hand and place the crimp in the crescent moon station of the pliers (photo 1). Press firmly. The goal is to have one wire on each side of the dent that this station puts into the crimp.

2. Turn the dented crimp sideways so the dent is centered between the pliers jaws in the oval station (photo 2).

3. Press down smoothly to fold the crimp at the dent (photo 3). For security, you may want to press the fold together with chain-nose pliers.

Peyote Stitch or Gourd Stitch

Tubular Peyote Stitch - Even Count

1. String an even number of beads that will fit around the object to be covered (figure 1, dark green beads). Tie the beads together into a ring, leaving a tiny bit of slack, and go through the first bead again (lower goldenrod line).

Figure 1

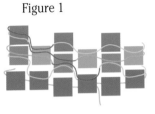

Note: the odd numbered beads make up row 2 and the even-numbered beads row 1.

2. For row 3, pick up a bead (medium green), skip the second strung bead, and go through the third. Pick up a bead, skip the next strung bead, and go through the next. Continue around. The last bead you pick up for the row will fit over the last strung bead (lower yellow line).

3. There is no clear "up" (raised) bead to sew through at the end of the row. Instead, you must "step up" by going through the first bead of the previous row and the first new bead of this row (bottom red line). You are now in position to add the first bead of row 4.

4. For row 4 (light green beads and second goldenrod line), pick up a bead and go through the second bead added on row 3. Continue around, adding beads over the row 2 beads and sewing through row 3 beads.

5. The last row 4 bead will go over the first strung bead and there won't be a clear attachment point after it. Step up by sewing through the first row 3 bead and the first row 4 bead (middle red line).

6. Pick up the first row 5 bead (blue and top yellow line) and go through the second row 4 bead. Repeat around in this manner. Then step up at the end of the row by sewing through the first bead added on the previous row, 4, and the first bead added on the row you are completing, 5 (top red line).

Notice that the step up moves one bead in the direction that you are sewing on each round.

Flat Peyote Stitch - Odd Count

1. Start with a stop bead. Then string an odd number of beads for rows 1 and 2. The odd-numbered beads form row 1 and the even-numbered beads make up row 2 and are shown half a bead higher in figure 2.

2. Pick up the first bead for row 3 (blue-green). Position it above the last bead strung and sew through the next-to-last bead.

3. Pick up a bead, skip a bead, and sew through the next bead. The last bead you pick up will sit over the first bead and there will be no following bead to which you can anchor it.

4. To fix its position you must work what is called "the hard turn," which really isn't as difficult as the name implies.

a. Sew through the first three beads strung in the original order – away from the stop bead (red line).

b. Sew through the bead above #3 toward the stop bead (red line).

c. Then continue through beads #2 and #1 (burgundy line).

d. Finally, sew through the last bead added on row 3 away from the stop bead (burgundy line). Your needle is exiting an "up" bead.

5. Work row 4 (light green) by picking up a bead and going through the next row 3 bead. Repeat across the row.

6. At the end of row 4 you will have anchored the last bead by sewing through the edge bead on row 3, so the turn to begin row 5 is easy. Just pick up a bead and sew through the last row 4 bead toward the stop bead.

7. Continue picking up row 5 beads and going through row 4 beads. The row will end like row 3 with no place to anchor the last bead (figure 2, arrow at top left).

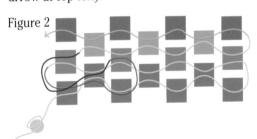

Figure 2

8. You can work a simpler "hard turn" at the end of all the odd-numbered rows after the first:

a. Sew through the edge bead and the bead diagonally below it away from the stop bead (figure 3, orange dot and line).

b. Turn and sew through the bead above the second bead then the edge bead you went through in step a (orange line to red line).

c. Now sew through the new bead at the end of the last row, working away from the stop bead (red line).

Figure 3

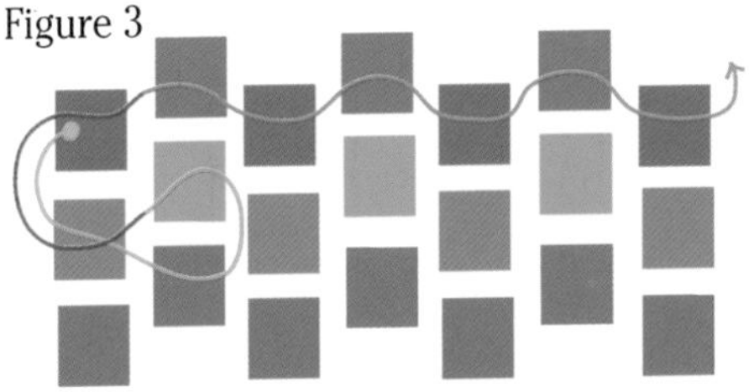

9. Work the easy turn at the end of even-numbered rows and the modified hard turn at the end of odd-numbered rows (the edge with the stop bead).

Ndebele Herringbone

Herringbone stitch works up quickly because you add two beads at a time. In other words, each stitch consists of two beads.

Figure 1

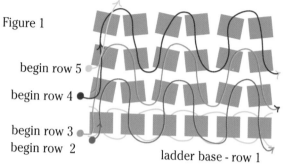

begin row 5

begin row 4

begin row 3
begin row 2

ladder base - row 1

Tubular Herringbone with a Ladder Base (figure 1)

The trick to successful tubular herringbone is the step up between rows. If you forget it, your tube will become skewed.

1. Start by making a ladder with an even number of beads (do not reinforce it). Then join the ladder into a ring (see "Brick stitch," p. 9, fig. 2).

2. For the first herringbone row but the second row of the piece, come out a ladder bead, pick up 2 beads. Sew down the second ladder bead (figure 1, red dot at left and line).

3. Sew up the third ladder bead, pick up 2 beads, and sew down the fourth ladder bead.

4. Repeat around until you have sewn down the last ladder bead (orange arrow at right).

5. To begin the next row (#3), you need to sew up through the first herringbone bead added. However, since your needle is pointing down through the last bead on the row below (orange arrow at right), you need to "step up" to reach the first row 2 bead. So sew up the first ladder bead and the first herringbone bead (orange dot at left).

6. With your needle exiting the first herringbone bead,

pick up 2 beads and sew down the second herringbone bead. Sew up the third and repeat around (orange line). You will end with your needle pointing down through the last row 2 bead (burgundy arrow).

7. Sew up the bead next to the one your needle is exiting (the first row 2 bead) and continue up the first bead of row 3 (burgundy dot and line).

8. For row 4, add pairs of beads over the pairs of row 3. At the end of the row you are going down the last row 3 bead (wheat arrow), so step up through the first row 3 and 4 beads to begin row 5 (wheat dot and line).

Note: If you look closely at the thread path in figure 1, you'll notice that the bead pairs of the top two rows separate from each other. Each new row pulls the pairs on the row below together. Normally, you join the pairs on the final row by working a ladder thread path through the beads (see figure 2 "Beaded Bead Bracelet" - page 16).

Tubular Herringbone with a Herringbone Base

1. Sew a stop bead on the thread about 6" (15cm) from the end. Then string 4 times as many beads as the number of stitches in your tube. (If you are working with a color pattern, notice how the beads stack in figure 3.) In this case, the tube will have 4 stitches, so string 16 beads (figure 2, orange line).

2. Sew back through #15 toward the start and pick up 2 beads for the third row of the first stitch. Be careful not to split any threads.

3. Sew through #14. Skip #13 and #12 and sew through #11. Pick up 2 beads and sew through #10.

4. Skip #9 and #8 and sew through #7. Pick up 2 beads and sew through #6.

5. Skip #5 and #4 and sew through #3. Pick up the 2 beads for the fourth stitch and sew through #2 and #1 (figure 2, red line).

Figure 3

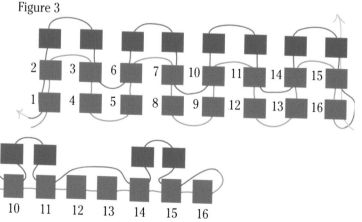

Figure 2

6. Pull both threads to gather the beads into 4 stitches 3 rows high. Pinch the beads between your thumb and index finger to prevent the strip from becoming twisted (figure 3).

7. To join the strip into a tube, sew up beads #16, #15, and the first new bead (wheat-colored line in figure 3).

8. Now work in regular tubular herringbone as shown in figure 1. Don't forget to step up to begin each new round.

Increasing Herringbone

An increase is completed in three rows of Ndebele Herringbone.

Figure 4

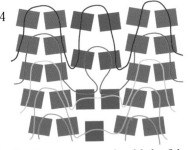

1. On the first increase round, add the 2 beads for the stitch before the increase and sew down the bead below the second bead of the new stitch. Pick up 1 bead. Sew up the first bead of the next stitch, add the two beads, and go down the next bead (figure 4, light orange line).

2. When you get to the increase point on the second row, add the 2 beads before the increase and go down the bead below. Pick up 2 beads and come up the first bead of the next stitch. Work the stitch (wheat line).

3. On the third row, transform the 2 increase beads with horizontal holes into a herringbone stitch. After making the stitch before the increase and sewing down the bead below, sew through the first increase bead. Pick up 2 beads and sew through the second increase bead. Then sew up the bead for the next regular stitch (red line).

The increase bead will tip up like a regular herringbone stitch.

Note: the increase will be slightly below the level of the other stitches but will even out to the same level in another row or two (burgundy line).

Brick Stitch

Ladder (figure 1)

1. Pick up 2 beads and sew through them again in the same order. Nudge them into a side-by-side position. The thread exits the bottom of bead #2.

2. Pick up bead #3. Sew down bead #2 (toward the thread) then back through bead #3 in the same direction as before (up). The thread exits its top.

3. Pick up bead #4 and sew up bead #3 (toward the thread). Then sew down bead #4.

Repeat step 2 for odd-number beads and step 3 for even-number beads.

Note: To firm up and reinforce your ladder, you can zigzag up and down beads back to bead #1 if you wish; do not do this for any of the projects in this book.

Joining a Ladder into a Tube (figure 2)

1. With the thread exiting the last ladder bead, bring the end and beginning beads of the ladder together. Make sure the ladder is not twisted.

2. If the thread is exiting the bottom of the last ladder bead, as shown here, sew bottom to top through the first ladder bead. (If the thread exits the top of the last bead, sew down the first.)

3. Sew back through the last ladder bead from top to bottom as shown.

4. Sew back up the first bead.

Brick Stitch (figures 3 and 4)

This method prevents thread from showing on the edge of the triangle. Each row is one bead shorter than the row below.

1. After completing a flat ladder with the thread exiting the top of the last bead, pick up 2 beads for the first brick stitch row.

2. Skip the nearest thread loop on the ladder (between the edge 2 beads) and sew under the loop between beads #2 and #3.

3. Sew back through the new beads, second bead first. Tighten the thread.

4. Sew through new bead #2 toward #1 so your needle is exiting the last bead added. As you tighten the thread, jiggle it to make the 2 beads assume a vertical position (figure 3, right edge).

5. Add the remaining beads on the row one at a time: Pick up the new bead, sew under the next thread loop on the row below. Sew back up the new bead. Tighten the thread so the bead stands upright (figure 3, beads #3 and 4 at top left).

Crystal Lattice Bracelets

Right-angle weave is one of my favorite stitches, but since the beads meet at right angles, too much of the holes show if you use Delicas. To counteract this problem, I adapted the stitch by placing a small bead between each of the large beads, creating an octagonal grid. The rows and stitches are connected to each other only through the large beads.

The bracelets on pages 10 and 12 look different, but both are woven in the same way. The pink Garden bracelet gets its feminine look with a ruffled edging. The tailored look of the sable bracelet comes from a geometric crystal arrangement. I used both round and bicone Swarovski crystals for a subtle texture, but use only one shape if you prefer.

SIZE: 6½" - 8" (16.5-20 cm)

MATERIALS

Pink Garden Bracelet

12-15g Delica beads, size 8/0 (metallic burgundy, DBL12)
7-10g Delica beads, size 10/0
        (raspberry-lined crystal AB, DBM56)
7g Delica beads, size 11/0 (rose-lined crystal, DB72)
2g Delica beads, size 11/0 (matte silver-lined pink, DB624)
44-54 Swarovski bicone crystals, 4mm, tourmaline
19-24 Swarovski bicone crystals, 4mm, rose satin
12-15 Swarovski bicone crystals, 4mm, ruby or fuchsia
Beading thread, Miyuki or K-O size B or Nymo D, pink
Beading needles, size 12
Sterling silver magnetic clasp
1½" - 2" (3.8-5cm) Sterling silver cable chain, fine gauge,
        for safety chain

HOW-TO

To weave either bracelet, start by weaving a strip of octagonal right-angle weave to the desired length. The bracelet should fit with ¼"-½" (6-13mm) of ease and the ends should meet.

Next applique the crystals over the grid spaces formed by the stitches, using doubled thread. Then attach the clasp.

Finish the Garden bracelet with a ruffle.

WEAVING THE BAND

The Garden Bracelet has three-stitch wide rows. Use the size 8/0 and 10/0 Delicas to weave the band with single thread, leaving a 24" (61cm) thread tail at both the beginning and the end for attaching the clasp.

Figure 1

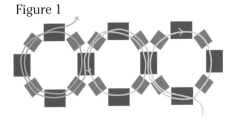

Pink Garden Bracelet

1. Begin by picking up 8 beads, alternating an 8/0 with a 10/0. Tie the beads into a firm ring using a surgeon's knot (see Knots on p. 6). Then go through the first 3 beads again to exit the second 8/0 (figure 1, yellow line).

2. Starting with a 10/0, alternate 10/0s and 8/0s. After the third 8/0, pick up a fourth 10 and go through the 8/0 you exited on the first stitch in the same direction.

3. Continue through the first 4 new beads, exiting the second 8/0 (figure 1, yellow-green line). Repeat step 2 to attach the third stitch to the second.

4. To position your needle so you can begin the second row, continue around through 6 beads of the last stitch to exit the 8/0 on the long side. The needle is pointing toward the first stitch (figure 1, green line).

Figure 2

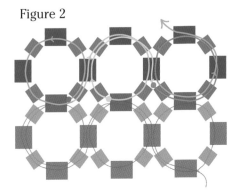

5. Alternate 10/0s and 8/0s and pick up 7 beads, beginning and ending with a 10/0. Sew through the 8/0 you exited on the row 1 stitch in the same direction as before (figure 2, blue dot and bright green line).

6. Continue through the first 10/0 and 8/0 of the new stitch. Alternately pick up 5 beads, beginning and ending with a 10/0 and sew through the 8/0 on the middle stitch of the first row toward the previous stitch (figure 2, yellow-green line). Finish the second stitch by picking up a final 10/0 and sewing through the side 8/0 on the first new stitch in the same direction that you exited it to begin stitch #2. Continue through the first 4 beads of stitch #2 (figure 2, yellow dot and line).

7. Pick up a 10/0 and sew through the top 8/0 of the third row 1 stitch to begin the third row 2 stitch (figure 2, khaki dot and line). Alternately pick up 5 beads, beginning and ending with a 10/0, and sew down the side 8/0 of the middle row 2 stitch (figure 2, khaki line).

8. Continue through the added 10/0 and the shared 8/0 at the top of the row 1 stitch* then the next 4 beads of the third row 2 stitch to exit the 8/0 at the top edge (figure 2, bright green line).

Notice that you alternate clockwise and counterclockwise circular thread paths. Turn the beadwork so it is in a comfortable direction as you work.

9. Repeat steps 5-8 to make each new row. Keep the thread pulled firm but not tight so the strip has a soft, drapey feel but almost no thread shows. (This bracelet has a pattern multiple of 8 rows, so stop at the desired length. Sable bracelet has 25 rows because that pattern multiple is 5 rows.)

10. To add thread, tie 2-3 pairs of half-hitches around the thread between beads, following the figure-8 thread path and exiting the same bead as the old thread. Work with the new thread, then end the old thread the same way. Leave the final tail for attaching the clasp.

Continue on pages 13 - 15

SIZE: 6½" - 8" (16.5-20 cm)
MATERIALS

Sable Bracelet

12-15g Delica beads, size 8/0 (dark bronze, DBL22)
7-10g Delica beads, size 10/0 (sable-lined crystal AB, DBM64)
5-7g Delica beads, size 11/0 (transparent brown, DB715)
40-49 Swarovski bicone crystals, 4mm, light Colorado topaz, SL
30-37 Swarovski bicone crystals, 4mm, aquamarine satin
30-38 Swarovski round crystals, 4mm, light sapphire champagne
Beading thread, Miyuki or K-O size B or Nymo D, dark brown
Beading needles, size 12
Sterling silver 4-loop slide clasp

REFER TO PAGES 1 - 14
FOR MORE DETAIL

WEAVING THE BAND
   The Sable Bracelet is four stitches wide. Use the size 8/0 and 10/0 Delicas to weave the band like the Garden bracelet, leaving a 24" (61cm) thread tail at both the beginning and the end.

Figure 3

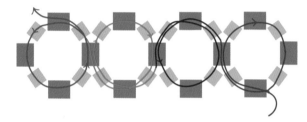

Sable Bracelet

1. Begin as in steps 1-3 of the Garden bracelet (figure 3, purple, dark blue, and light blue lines). Then repeat step 2 again to add the fourth stitch.
2. Continue through the first 2 beads to exit the 8/0 on the long edge. The needle is pointing away from the first stitch (figure 3, blue line).

Figure 4

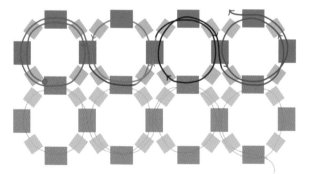

3. Repeat step 5 (p. 11). Then sew through the first 6 beads of the new stitch (figure 4, blue dot and line).
4. Pick up a 10/0 and sew through the edge 8/0 of the second row 1 stitch to begin the second row 2 stitch (figure 4, purple line). Pick up 5 beads of alternating size, beginning and ending with a 10/0, and sew down the side 8/0 of the first stitch on row 2.

5. Continue through the added 10/0 and the shared 8/0 at the top of the second stitch on row 1. Then sew up the next 2 beads of the new stitch to exit the 8/0 at the open side (figure 4, light blue line).

6. Alternately pick up 5 beads beginning and ending with a 10/0. Go through the top 8/0 of the third row 1 stitch. Pick up a 10/0 and go through the side 8/0 of the previous row 2 stitch. Continue through the first 4 beads of the third new stitch (figure 4, dark blue line). Work the fourth stitch like the second stitch. Continue counterclockwise around the beads of the fourth stitch to exit the top 8/0 (figure 4, blue line).

7. Work the first 3 stitches of row 3 like row 2 of the Garden bracelet, but going in the opposite direction (steps 5-8*, p. 11). For the fourth stitch, sew up the 2 edge beads of the third stitch. Pick up 5 beads, beginning and ending with a 10/0. Sew up through the top 8/0 of the fourth row 2 stitch, pick up a 20/0, and continue through the 8/0 that connects stitches 3 and 4. Continue through 2 more beads of the fourth stitch to end coming through the top bead of the fourth stitch, pointing away from the band.

8. Repeat rows 2-3 to desired length.

Figure 5

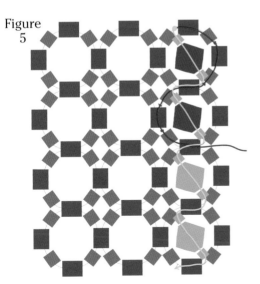

Garden and Sable Bracelets continued

ADDING CRYSTAL EMBELLISHMENTS

Work one row of crystals at a time along the length of the bracelet.

On the Garden bracelet, the pattern repeats every eight rows, and on the sable bracelet it repeats every 5 rows.

For security, begin and end a new doubled thread for each of the rows.

1. Begin the first edge row with a yard or meter of doubled thread.

Sew into the third 8/0 from the end toward the other edge and sew up around the inner half of the second stitch in a clockwise direction, tying 1-2 pairs of half hitches between beads. Exit the second 8/0 from the end and sew counterclockwise around the outside edge of the first stitch tying 1-2 pairs of half hitches. Exit the end 8/0 of the row with the needle pointing toward the other side (the left – figure 5, dark gray line to yellow dot).

Chart 2 - Sable Bracelet

Chart 1 - Garden Bracelet

2. See chart 1 for the garden bracelet and chart 2 for the sable bracelet.

Add the first row of crystals working down the right-hand vertical row of the chart. When you reach the end of the chart row repeat it again from the top until you have appliqued a crystal over the last stitch on the right-hand edge of the band.

3. To add each crystal pick up an 11/0 Delica (I used rose for the garden bracelet), the appropriate crystal (tourmaline for the garden bracelet; aquamarine for the sable bracelet) and another 11/0 Delica.

4. Sew right to left through the next horizontal 8/0. Continue adding crystals as in steps 3 and 4 (figure 5, yellow dot and line) until you finish the last stitch of the edge row. End the thread in the row the same way you started it.

5. Start a new double thread in the next row from the edge at the beginning end as in step 1. Then add the second row of crystals and end the thread. Repeat for third (and fourth) row of crystals.

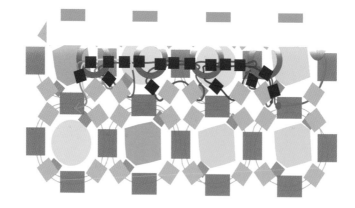

ADDING THE CLASP

Garden Bracelet

1. To attach a magnetic clasp, thread a needle with the thread tail at one end of the bracelet.

Pull the needle to a little past half the length of the thread so it will be doubled.

2. Weave to the second or third 8/0 from the end on the underside of the middle row.

The clasp part should fall just short of the edge of the band.

String an 11/0, the clasp, the end link of the safety chain, and an 11/0 and sew back through the 8/0 toward the first 11/0 strung.

Reinforce the attachment once or twice. End the thread securely.

3. Repeat with the thread tail at the other end, positioning the clasp at the second or third 8/0 from the end so that when the clasp is closed the ends of the band meet.

Make sure that the ends of the safety chain are on the same side of the closed clasp.

Sable Bracelet

The goal is to have the closed slide clasp completely concealed under the ends of the bracelet so that the ends butt together.

1. Double the thread tail as in the Garden Bracelet step 1 and weave around the end stitch on the underside to exit the second 8/0 from the end pointing toward the other edge of the bracelet (figure 6, dark gray line to magenta dot).

Pick up 2-3 size 11/0s, sew down the first clasp loop, and go through the upper 10/0 to the left of the 8/0 you exited (figure 6, magenta dot and line). Repeat the thread path (the repeats are not shown in figure 6).

2. Come back up the first 2 11/0s. Pick up 4 11/0s, sew down the second clasp loop, and go through the 10/0 to the left of the 10/0 you used in step 1 (figure 6, purple line).

3. Come up the first clasp loop and repeat the thread path. Then go through the first 3 11/0s of the second stitch again. Pick up 4 11/0s and go down the third clasp loop. Sew through the fifth, then fourth 10/0 (left to right – figure 6, blue line).

4. Come up the second clasp loop. Repeat the thread path. Repeat through the first 3 11/0s of the third stitch, pick up 4 11/0s and sew down the fourth clasp loop. Go left to right through the sixth 10/0. Then come up the second of the 11/0s on this stitch (figure 6, red line to yellow dot). Repeat the thread path.

5. Finally, sew through the second and third 11/0s of the fourth stitch again. Pick up 2 11/0s and sew left to right through the seventh 10/0 (figure 6, yellow line to green dot). Come up the fourth 11/0 of the fourth stitch and through the fourth clasp loop from bottom to top. Go through the 2 beads of the fifth stitch (figure 6, green line). Repeat the thread path. Then end the thread securely in the beadwork (figure 6, green arrow).

6. Close the clasp to attach the first loop of the second half. Repeat step 1. Open the clasp, reinforce the first stitch, and repeat steps 2-5.

Figure 7

MAKING THE GARDEN BRACELET RUFFLE

1. Weave in a new 2-yard (1.8m) single thread so that the thread is exiting the 8/0 on the end and pointing toward the edge you will ruffle first.

Continue through the 10/0 toward the edge (figure 7, yellow dot).

2. Row 1: Pick up 2 10/0s, position them above the first edge 8/0, and go through the 10/0 to its left.

Pick up a rose-colored 11/0 and sew through the next 10/0 on the edge (figure 7, yellow line to blue dot and photo 1).

Repeat this step along the entire edge (figure 7, light blue dot at left).

3. Row 2: To begin, sew through the end 8/0 then through the crystal and its 11/0s.

Reverse direction, sewing around the right-angle weave stitch to exit the end 8/0 and the 10/0 to its right (figure 7, light blue line). Then sew through the last new 10/0 toward the starting end of the ruffle.

4. Work the second row in peyote stitch, adding a rose 11/0 after each bead added on the first row (figure 7, blue line).

5. Row 3: To begin, go clockwise through 5 beads of the end stitch then the crystal and its 11/0s to turn.

Continue back through the first 10/0 of the end stitch, the first 10/0 of row 1, and the last new 11/0 of row 2 (figure 7, blue line to light blue line and green dot on right).

6. Pick up 3 rose 11/0s, 1 pink 11/0, and 3 rose 11/0s. Sew through the rose 11/0 between the next pair of 10/0s (photo 2). Repeat to the end (figure 7, green line). Then end this thread securely in the bracelet.

7. Repeat steps 1-6 on the other long edge of the bracelet.

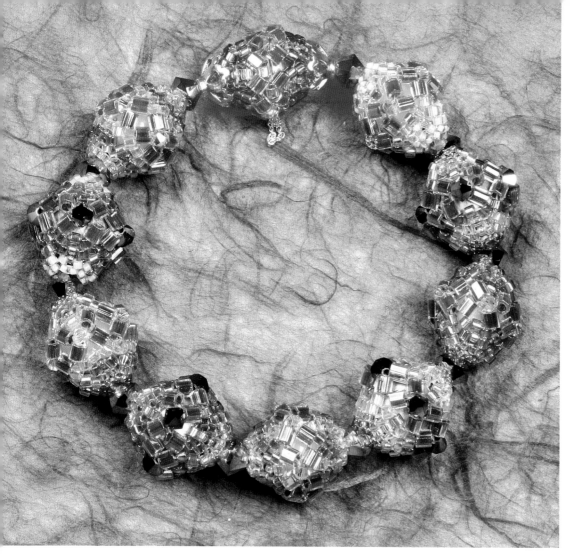

beads: wooden beads, which I use for the core, are hardly ever the size stated on the package.

For the beads made with 4mm crystals I used wooden beads labeled 10mm, but they are really about 11.6mm in diameter and 11.3mm in length. When I used 3mm crystals, I had to find smaller core beads and used 10.25mm stone beads, labeled 10mm.

Sometimes I file or sand the wooden core bead a bit smaller in both dimensions.

Glorious Beaded Bead Bracelet

Ndebele Herringbone
see pages 8 - 9

I love developing beaded beads, and I love Ndebele herringbone stitch, but for the longest time I couldn't figure out how to use it successfully for beaded beads. Beaded beads should be symmetrical at the hole.

Then I had a wonderful ah ha! moment! By starting my herringbone beads in the center,

I can make the second half a mirror image of the first.

Adding crystals between the stitches on the circumference row was a natural, and the graduated sizes of Delicas makes the construction a cinch. Since then I've been creating a huge variety of herringbone beaded bead sizes and shapes.

These beads are a delight to make.

Figure 1

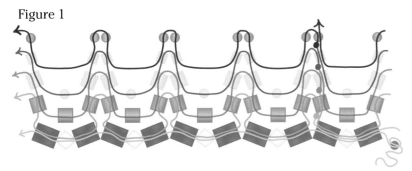

MATERIALS

You'll need to make a bead or two more than you would suppose. Because of their size, the inside circumference of the bracelet is markedly smaller than its length. My 7" (17.8cm) bracelet is 8½" (21.6cm) long.

5-7 Wood or stone beads (light color), 10mm

4-6 Wood beads, 11.5mm approximately (use large 10mm or sand down 12mm)

7-10g Delica beads, size 8/0 (medium-blue-lined crystal AB cuts, DBL58C)

5-7g Delica beads, size 10/0 (transparent Capri blue AB, DBM177)

5-7g Delica beads, size 10/0 (medium-blue-lined crystal AB, DBM58)

5-7g Delica beads, size 10/0 (transparent seafoam AB, DBM83)

5g Delica beads, size 11/0 (transparent sky blue AB, DB176)

5g Delica beads, size 11/0 (light blue-lined crystal, DB78)

3-5g Miyuki seed beads, size 15/0 (transparent Capri blue AB, 291)

3-5g Miyuki seed beads, size 15/0 (transparent light blue AB, 260)

3-5g Miyuki seed beads, size 15/0 (light blue-lined crystal, 2207)

10-14 Swarovski bicone crystals, 6mm, jet AB 2X

20-30 Swarovski bicone crystals, 4mm, jet AB 2X

25-35 Swarovski bicone crystals, 3mm, crystal AB

Beading thread, Miyuki or K-O size B light blue or Fireline

Beading needles, size 12 or 13

Sterling silver magnetic clasp

1½"-2" (3.8-5cm) Sterling silver cable chain, fine gauge, for safety chain

2 Sterling silver bead caps, approx. 9.3 x 5.3mm

14" (35.5cm) Flexible beading wire, size .014-.019

2 Sterling silver crimp tubes, 1 x 2mm

Silver acrylic paint

Toothpicks and corrugated cardboard box

TIP: Before starting to bead, I always paint my wooden beads with either silver or gold acrylic paint. I make a small dish shape with a scrap of aluminum foil, put the beads in it, and squirt some paint over them. I roll them around in the paint with a toothpick until they are completely covered. Then I insert a toothpick in a bead and stick the other end between the corrugations of a box with the toothpick horizontal.

Symmetrical Ndebele Herringbone

HOW-TO

These beads have 5 herringbone stitches with a floating fill-in bead between most of the stitches. Be extremely careful not to split the thread on the first 3 rows. Combine bead colors in any pleasing pattern.

1. Thread a needle with 1½ -2 yd. (1.4-1.8m) of beading thread and work with it single. String a scrap 15/0 bead to the center of the thread and go through it again to make a stop bead.

2. To make a small beaded bead with a 10mm core, string an 8/0, a 3mm crystal, and an 8/0. Repeat 4 more times. Then sew through the first 3 beads to join them into a ring. Leave about an inch (2.5cm) of slack in the ring for row 1 (figure 1, yellow line to orange dot and photo 2).

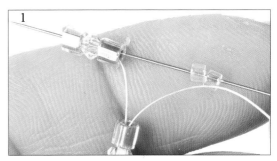

1

3. To begin row 2 (figure 1, orange dot), pick up 2 size 10/0s (photo 2) and sew through the next 3 beads on the ring. Repeat around 4 more times then continue through the first 10/0 (figure 1, orange line to dark orange dot). Most of the slack in the ring thread will have been used as the beads pull into upside down V-shaped pairs. If you didn't leave enough, you may have to move the stop bead down the thread to bring more thread into the ring.

2

4. For row 3, pick up 2 size 10/0s and sew through the second 10/0 of row 2 toward the 8/0 (photo 3).

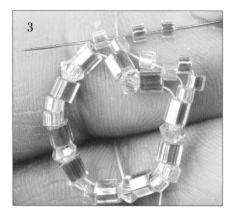

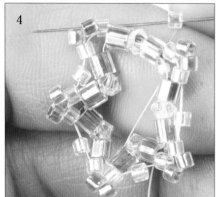

Pick up 1 size 10/0 for a floating bead between stitches and sew up through the first bead of the next pair of row 2 10/0s. Repeat this step 4 more times, ending by picking up a floating 10/0 and sewing up the first 10/0 on row 2 and the first 10/0 on row 3 (photo 4 and figure 1, dark orange line to red dot).

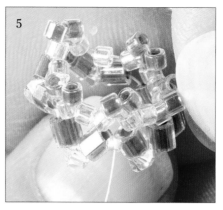

5. Adjust the tension of the starting tail to shape the piece into deep zigzags with as little thread showing on row 1 as possible (photo 5).

6. Row 4 consists of pairs of size 11/0 Delicas with a size 15/0 or an 11/0 Delica for the float beads (figure 1, red line to maroon dot).

7. Use pairs of 15/0s with no float beads for the fifth and final row. End by going through the first 15/0 of the round (figure 1, maroon line).

Figure 3

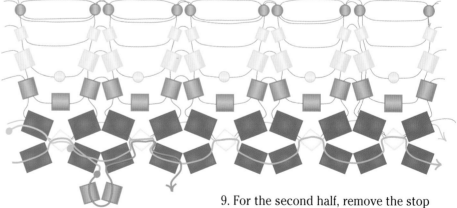

Figure 2

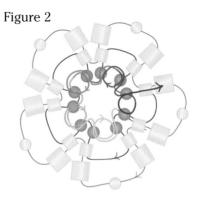

8. Close the end of the bead cover by sewing down the second 15/0, up the third, and down the second again. Sew up the third 15/0 and down the fourth (figure 2, yellow line). Then go up the fifth and back down the fourth.

Repeat this pattern around the final row to pull the stitches together.

Then weave through a few beads and tie a pair of half hitches (see Knots, p. 6) at least twice. Go through a few beads after the last knot pair before clipping the thread.

9. For the second half, remove the stop bead and thread a needle on the other end of the starting thread. You will work this side in the opposite direction from the first. Sew through the nearest 8/0 and crystal (figure 3, yellow dot at left).

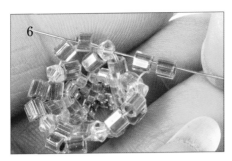

10. For row 1, pick up 2 size 8/0s and go through the next crystal. Repeat around 4 more times (figure 3, orange dot and line) and end by sewing through the first crystal and the first new 8/0 (photo 6). Tighten the thread so the 8/0s form inverted Vs.

11. Repeat step 3 to work row 2 (figure 3, dark orange dot). Then insert a 10mm core bead so that its widest part is at the level of the crystals and the hole is vertical.

12. Repeat steps 4-8 above. If the core bead's hole is not in line with the beaded cover's hole, use a size 10 beading needle or an awl to turn the core bead into position.

4. On row 5 use pairs of 15/0s with a 15/0 floating bead between each pair. Then close the end as in step 8.

5. Begin the second half as in steps 9 and 10. Then repeat rows 2-5, inserting the 11.5mm core bead after row 2.

CLASP COVER

One of the coolest things about this bracelet is that the clasp is concealed by two half-bead covers so it looks as though it's just another bead, making the bracelet appear seamless.

1. Start with a yard (1m) of thread and place a stop bead about 6" (15cm) from the end.

2. Work like the first half of the smaller bead, steps 1-8, but use 10/0s instead of crystals on the first row and float 15/0s on row 4.

3. After tightening the starting end, remove the stop bead and weave and knot the tail securely into the beadwork.

4. Make a second identical piece.

clasp parts near the end of a length of flexible beading wire. Thread the tail back through the crimp and draw it into a small loop with a very little ease. Flatten the crimp with chain-nose pliers.

3. Thread one of the clasp covers onto the wire, wide end first and cover its hole with a bead cap, strung wide end first. Then string a 6mm crystal.

4. String your beaded beads, placing a 6mm crystal after each. End with a 6mm crystal and check the bracelet for size. Add or remove beaded beads as needed.

Finally, string a bead cap, narrow end first, the other clasp cover, narrow end first, a crimp, the other end of the safety chain, then the other part of the magnetic clasp.

5. Tighten the beads on the wire so the 6mm crystals sit down in the holes of the beaded beads, which prevents them from wobbling.

Thread the wire tail back through the crimp, clasp cover, bead cap, 6mm crystal, and the end beaded bead.

6. All bracelets need ease so they will fit around your wrist softly, but allowing enough ease won't be a problem here.

The trick is to get the beads as snug as you can before crimping so there isn't too much ease.

When the wire is tight, gently push the clasp cover down over the clasp part to open barely enough space between it and the bead cap so you can get the tips of your chain-nose pliers in to flatten the crimp.

When the bracelet is open, you should have about 4-5mm of ease, but when the magnets are joined, everything should fit snugly together.

Figure 4

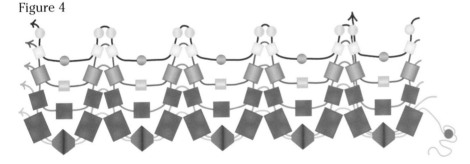

Larger Bead

1. The larger bead (figure 4) also has 5 rows on each side, but use 4mm crystals in the starting row, steps 1 and 2, rather than 3mm crystals.

2. Work rows 2 and 3 as in steps 3-5.

3. Work row 4 as in step 6, but use 11/0 Delicas for the floating beads.

STRINGING

1. Arrange your beads in the desired order. I alternated small and large beads, beginning and ending with a small bead.

2. When you're happy with the arrangement, thread a 1mm crimp, one end of the safety chain, and one of the magnetic

My first peyote stitch project was an odd-count tube similar to this necklace. Odd-count tubular peyote is the easiest form of tubular peyote because there is no definite beginning or end of a round – you just keep going round and round until the tube is the desired length – so it's ideal for a spiral pattern.

Tubular Peyote Stitch
see page 7

Golden Spiral

There's one trick to remember to keep your spiral perfect: pick up the same kind of bead as the bead you just went through. Using sizes 8/0, 10/0, and 11/0 Delica beads gives this rope its ridged texture. It would be smooth (and kind of boring) if I'd used only one size bead.

I made my rope one-and-a-half times the desired length of my necklace so I could cross and twist the ends in front and button them to the opposite sides. If you prefer a simple necklace, feel free to make your rope the desired length and sew a button to one end and a loop to the other.

I've had the vintage gilded, carved wood buttons I used in the necklace at left for so long that I don't remember where they came from, but it wasn't hard to find wonderful commercial buttons at a sewing store for the other necklace. I had fun making it by using related different color size 8/0 Delicas for each half. When the ends cross and twist, the necklace front is more interesting.

MATERIALS
20-25g Delica beads, size 8/0 (shiny gold, DBL34)
OR10-13g Delica beads, each of 2 colors, size 8/0: (shiny gold and black-lined light topaz AB, DBL89C)
15-20g Delica beads, size 10/0 (dark blue iris, DBM5)
10g Delica beads, size 11/0 (med. blue luster, DB58)
Beading thread, Miyuki or K-O size B or D or Nymo D, medium brown (Hint: I find that when I'm using a variety of bead colors, medium brown thread hides best.)
Beading needles, size 10 or 12
2 Large decorative buttons, shank or 2-hole, ¾"-1¼" diameter (19-32mm)

WEAVING THE ODD-COUNT TUBE
Tension is important to the wearability of this necklace. Work with a firm but soft tension so the tube bends easily but there are no obvious thread gaps.

1. To start tubular peyote, thread a needle with a long but manageable length of thread and work with it single. Leaving a 4"- 6" (10-15cm) thread tail, string the following bead pattern to make up the first two rows:

   1 size 8/0, 4 size 10/0, 4 size 11/0, and 2 size 10/0 (11 beads in total).

Figure 1

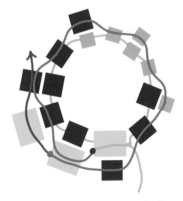

2. Tie the beads into a moderately firm ring with a surgeon's knot (see Knots on p. 6) and go through the 8/0 bead toward the 4 size 10/0s (figure 1, dark red dot).

3. Pick up the same kind of bead as the one you went through, an 8/0 (remember, this is the trick for maintaining a spiral pattern), skip the first 10/0 and go through the second.

4. Pick up a 10/0, skip the third 10/0 on the ring and go through the fourth.

5. Pick up a 10/0, skip the first 11/0 on the ring and go through the second.

6. Pick up an 11/0, skip the third 11/0 and go through the fourth.

7. Pick up an 11/0, skip the first of the 2 size 10/0s and go through the second.

8. Pick up a 10/0 and go through the 8/0 you added to begin the round (figure 1, med. brown line to red dot).

Figure 2

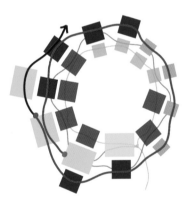

9. On subsequent rounds, go through each bead you added on the previous round, which is a bit higher than the next bead, picking up the same kind of bead as the one you went through (you'll add 6 beads on each round), until the tube is the desired length (figure 2). Mine are 25" (64cm) long.

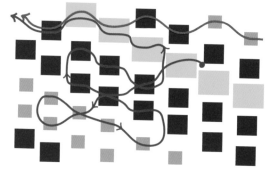

1

Because of the varied bead sizes, it may be difficult to see the places where you add the second 11/0 and the single 10/0.

You'll find that the size 11/0 Delicas are lower than the 10/0s on either side, and you may miss them if you aren't careful, but remember that you need to add 2 size 11/0s and that the second goes on top of a size 10/0. The single 10/0 goes over an 8/0 (photo 1).

Figure 3

ENDING AND ADDING THREAD

1. When you have about 6" (15cm) of thread left on the needle, it's time to add thread. Leave the short thread and needle in place (figure 3, gray line) and thread a new needle.

2. Starting a few rows from the end, weave the new thread (figure 3, red line) diagonally through 3-4 beads, heading toward the starting end of the rope.

3. Go through the bead above the last one you went through in the opposite direction and weave diagonally down through 4-5 beads, crossing the first thread diagonal.

4. Weave another diagonal upward, crossing the first and going through 2-3 beads. Figure 3 shows another downward cross through 3 beads.

5. Finally, weave diagonally up through beads until you reach the last row worked and follow the thread path to exit the same bead that the short thread is exiting in the same direction (figure 3, top left).

6. Resume peyote stitch with the new thread. When you have worked 5-6 rounds, end the old thread in the new work with about 3 crosses the same way you started the new thread.

7. End the starting thread tail in this manner, too.

MAKING THE CLOSURE

1. Using doubled thread, sew one button 6" (15cm) from one end of the tube and the other 7" (17.8cm) from the other end.

2. Weave a doubled thread into the tube with at least three crosses and exit a size 8/0 Delica at the desired length from the end.

If your buttons have 2 holes, string a 10/0 bead, go through the first hole, string 1-5 size 10/0s to reach the second hole, and sew down it. Pick up a 10/0 and sew through the same 8/0 on the tube toward the first 10/0 (photo 2).

3. Reinforce the thread path at least twice more. Then end the thread by sewing at least 3 diagonals in the tube.

4. Attach the second button the same way at the desired distance from the other end of the tube.

5. If your buttons have a shank, file off any rough edges, then sew the shank to the desired 8/0, reinforcing the attachment at least 3 times.

6. To weave a button loop at each end of the tube, start with a single thread about a yard (1m) long and weave it securely into the tube with crosses, exiting the last 8/0.

7. String enough 10/0s to make a loop that fits easily but not loosely over a button. Test the size by going through the first of the 4 size 10/0s at the end of the tube. When the loop is the right length, sew through all 4 of the end 10/0s, the 8/0 from which you began, and all the loop beads. Continue through the 4 size 10/0s on the tube, the 8/0, and the first loop bead.

FINISHING:

8. Using 10/0s, weave a row of peyote stitch onto the loop beads: pick up a bead, skip a loop bead, and go through the next loop bead all the way around the loop (photo 3).

If your loop has an even number of beads, you'll add a bead over the last loop bead. If it has an odd number of beads, you'll sew through the last loop bead.

Whichever the case, continue through the tube 10/0s, the 8/0, and the first loop bead.

9. Finish the loop by picking up 2 size 11/0s, setting them between the first pair of 10/0s on the loop and sewing through the next single loop bead (photo 4). Repeat around.

Then end the thread in the tube with at least 3 crosses.

10. Make a loop at the other end of the tube.

TIP: To wear the necklace, cross the ends, wrap them around each other once or twice; button the loops to the opposite buttons.

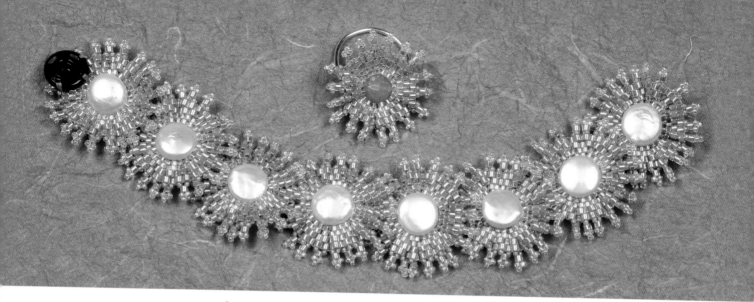

Morning Glory Jewelry

Brick Stitch
see page 9

I know that not everyone loves brick stitch as much as I do. In fact, I wasn't too crazy about it until I started discovering its versatility, both alone and in combination with other stitches.

Years ago, I picked up a technique from Ella Johnson Bentley for ringing a centerpiece bead with thread and then working a brick-stitch ladder off that thread. That technique forms the base of the ring, bracelet, earrings and necklace here.

Ringing spherical beads is easier than flat beads because the beadwork tends to shift on the latter. But sewing beads across the backs of the flat pearls I used for my bracelet makes the beadwork stay put around the edge.

MATERIALS

Bracelet and Ring

10g Delica beads, size 10/0 (turquoise-lined crystal AB, DBM79)
7g Delica beads, size 11/0 (transparent seafoam AB, DB83)
5g Miyuki seed beads, size 15/0 (turquoise-lined crystal, 2208)
5g Miyuki seed beads, size 15/0 (transparent seafoam AB, 2212)
7-10 Coin pearls, 10-11mm, white
1 Swarovski round crystal, 8mm, Pacific opal
3" (7.6cm) Sterling silver round wire, half hard, 18- or 20-gauge
6" (15cm) Sterling silver round wire, half hard, 16-gauge
Beading thread, Miyuki or K-O size B, pale blue
Beading needles, size 12 or 13
Large snap, size 3

MATERIALS

Necklace and earrings

12-15g Delica beads, size 10/0 (cream-lined crystal AB, DBM52)
7-10g Delica beads, size 11/0 (coral-lined crystal AB, DB54)
5-7g Miyuki seed beads, size 15/0 (coral-pink-lined crystal, 2199)
15 Glass pearls, 12mm, mauve
12 Glass pearls, 8mm, white
Beading thread, Miyuki or K-O size B, cream or flesh
Beading needles, size 12 or 13
2 Swarovski bicone crystals, 8mm, peach
36" (.9m) Gold-filled round wire, 20- or 22-gauge
   (since the wire won't show, you can use silver if you prefer)
24" (61cm) Flexible beading wire, size .014-.018
2 Sterling silver tube crimps, 2mm
Complementary sterling silver clasp
   (mine with a coin pearl is from PacificSilverworks.com)
Gold-filled earring findings
2 Gold-filled head pins

1

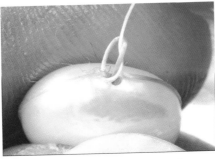

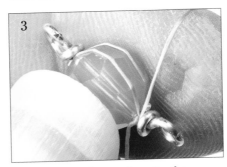

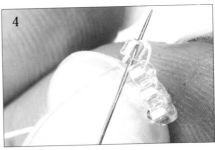

MAKING THE THREAD BASE

1. For the necklace, earrings, and ring cut a 2"- 3" (5-7.6cm) piece of wire, depending on the size of the bead, and make a small wrapped loop with a single wrap at one end of the wire. String the centerpiece bead onto the wire and make a single-wrapped loop against the bead, leaving a tiny amount of play.

Use gold-filled wire for the necklace and earrings (but since it won't show, silver is fine). Use 18- or 20-gauge silver wire for the ring.

2. Holding the loops on each bead with two pairs of pliers, adjust them to be in the same plane.

3. The wrapped thread base needs a tiny bit of ease so you can sew under it without scratching the bead.

For the coin pearl bracelet, which has no wire, cut a 2 yard (1.8m) length of thread and work with it single.

Sew through the pearl, leaving a 4" (10cm) thread tail. Carry the thread around one edge of the pearl back to the tail and knot the working thread and tail together with a square knot (see Knots, p. 6).

This knot doesn't have to be right at the hole because you can pull it to the hole (but not inside the hole) with the next thread pass (photo 1).

4. Go through the pearl again and set the thread around the other edge to the tail. Tie this wrap to the first at the hole with a half hitch knot (photo 2).

If there is room in the pearl for two more thread passes, do so, securing each at the hole.

5. For the beads on wires, tie the thread securely to the wire between the wrap and the bead, using a surgeon's knot. Take the thread to the other end and wrap it around the wire between the wrap and bead. Wrap on the other side and secure again at the starting end. Repeat to double the thread wraps (photo 3). Secure the final wrap to the wraps on the other side of the wire with a half hitch.

Figure 1

pick up 2 beads, stitch it all back to front under the thread wrap as close to the center bead's hole as you can (figure 1, light blue line). Sew through the second bead then the first (figure 1, medium blue line). Now sew through the second bead again toward the first (figure 1, purple line). As you tighten the thread, jiggle it to get the beads to stand up with their holes vertical. Push them against the center bead's hole.

2. For the remaining beads on the ladder, pick up 1 bead, sew under the thread wrap back to front. Then sew through the bead again in the same direction (figure 1, teal line and photo 4).

Repeat around, squeezing beads tightly against each side of the bottom hole. On the beads with wrapped loops, fill as close to each side of the wire as possible, and always position the beads in front of the wire (photo 5).

3. You will have 18 beads on the 8mm glass pearls and crystal, 24 on the 12mm glass pearls, and 22 or 24 on the coin pearls. Put half on each side.

When you near the end of the round, count to make sure you will have an even number of beads. If not, squeeze the beads more tightly together to add an extra bead, or spread them a bit to omit one bead.

Bead size	Round 1 11/0	Round 2 11/0	Round 3 10/0	Round 4 10/0
12mm glass pearls (8 increases per round)	24	32	40	48
8mm beads (6 increases per round)	18	24	30	36
First increase after		2nd bead	3rd bead	4th bead
Increase after every		3rd stitch	4th stitch	5th stitch
Work 1 bead stitch after the last increase to finish each round.				
Coin pearls (6 increases per round)	22-24	28-30	34-36	40-42
First increase after		3rd bead	4th bead	5th bead
Increase after every		4th stitch	5th stitch	6th stitch

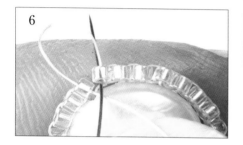

4. End the round by sewing down the first bead and back up the last bead to join the ends (photo 6 and figure 1, magenta line).

5. Work round 2 with 11/0 Delicas and rounds 3 and 4 with 10/0s.

Each of these rounds also requires increases as prescribed in the chart – 6 increases per round on the coin pearls and 8mm beads and 8 per round on the 12mm glass pearls.

Note: There is some irregularity in the increase pattern for the coin pearls because their circumferences vary slightly.

Exception: When bead count is the lower number, the sixth increase goes after the last bead of each round (the 3rd on round 2, the 4th on round 3, and the 5th on round 4).

When bead counts are the higher number, add 1 bead on each round after the last increase.

Figure 2

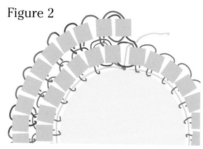

6. Use size 11/0 Delicas for round 2 and begin it with 2 beads. Skip the thread loop between the first and last bead of round 1 and sew under the thread loop between beads #1 and #2.

Complete the stitch as described in step 1 (figure 2, magenta and teal lines). Add the remaining beads of the round one at a time, sewing under each thread loop between the beads of round 1.

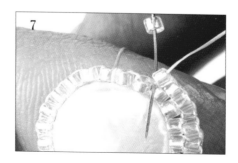

7. On the coin pearls, the first increase is made after adding the third bead. Pick up a bead, and sew under the same thread loop to which you attached the previous bead (photo 7).

Then sew back up the increase bead (figure 2, upper dark blue line).

8. According to the chart the remaining increases are placed in the same space as the fourth bead added (figure 2, lower dark blue line). If your first round has 24 beads, the sixth increase will go in the space before the last thread loop of the round below. Add the last bead and join the round as in step 4.

Note: If the first round had 22 beads, There will be spaces for only 3 beads after the fifth increase, so add the sixth increase after the last bead. Then join it to the first bead.

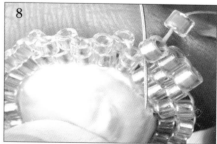

loop to which you add the increase beads, and the beads will ruffle even more (photo 8).

10. Work round 4 with size 10/0 Delicas, taking special care to end with an even number of beads.

Figure 3

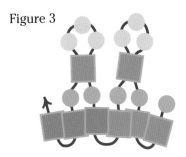

ADDING THE PICOT POINTS

I worked three slightly different picot patterns.

Bracelet and Ring

1. Exiting a Delica on round 4, pick up a 15/0 turquoise bead (D), a 10/0 Delica, and 3 size 15/0 seafoam beads (L).

Sew down the 10/0 toward the D. Pick up 1D, and sew down the next round 4 bead. Tighten the picot and adjust the top beads to form a triangle (figure 3).

2. Sew up the next round 4 bead and make another picot. Since some of the round 4 beads are behind their neighbors, be careful not to skip any of them.

3. When you've added a picot to the last pair of 10/0s, end the thread securely in the beadwork with 2-3 pairs of half hitches.

Necklace and Earrings

1. To bring the color at the center of each flower back to the outer edge, work the following picot pattern in each pair of 10/0 Delicas:

Pick up an 11/0 Delica, a 10/0, and 3 size 15/0 coral pink beads. Sew back down the 10/0, pick up another 11/0 Delica, and sew into the adjacent bead on the fourth round (figure 4).

Figure 5

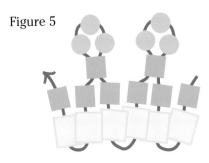

2. For a more delicate, shorter picot on the earrings, substitute an 11/0 Delica for the 10/0 on the necklace picots (figure 5).

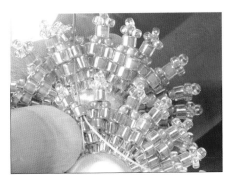

ASSEMBLING THE BRACELET

My bracelet has 8 flowers and measures 7" (17.8cm), but the size of the flowers means that it will fit about ½" (1.3cm) snugger than the length indicates.

You can end and add thread to join each flower or use a single yard-long (1m) thread and work it through the beads to reach the joining spot for the next flower.

1. Decide which side of each coin pearl flower should show. Weave a thread securely into the first flower, exiting a round 4 bead in line with one of the pearl's holes on the right side, pointing toward the pearl.

2. Sew into a round 4 bead on the second flower in line with the pearl hole but on the wrong side.

Go from the edge toward the pearl. Continue through the same bead of the first flower in the same direction (photo 9).

Don't tighten the thread all the way.

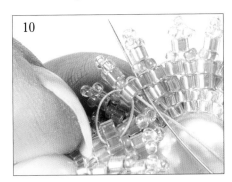

10

3. Sew through the adjacent row 4 bead on the first flower toward the picots (photo 10).

4. Sew through the adjacent row 4 bead on the second flower toward the picots (photo 11).

5. Tighten the thread and reinforce the 2 stitches. Then weave through beads on the second flower to exit a row 4 bead as in step 1 on the right side directly opposite the first join.

6. Continue in this manner joining flowers so they overlap. Pay careful attention to right and wrong sides.

7. When the bracelet is the desired length, sew the female part of the snap to the first flower on the right side as close to its edge as possible. Sew the male part of the snap to the wrong side at the end of the last flower, partially overlapping the pearl (photo 12).

8. I tried all sorts of things, including glue, to keep the pearls from rotating.

Finally, I solved the problem by sewing a grid of 2 lines of 11/0 Delicas horizontally and vertically behind the pearls anchored to round 1 (photo 13).

ASSEMBLY

ASSEMBLING THE EARRINGS
Make two 8mm pearl flowers.

1. Thread an 8mm peach crystal on a head pin and start a medium-sized wrapped loop above it, leaving space for 2 wraps.

Before wrapping, attach the loop to one of the loops on a small pearl flower.

2. Open the loop on an earwire and attach it to the other loop on the pearl flower. Close it tightly.

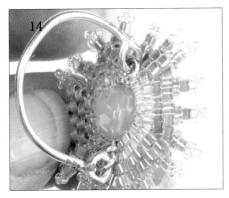

ASSEMBLING THE RING

A ring mandrel is helpful, but you can use your finger and a small cylindrical object to bend the wire for the ring body.

1. Bend the 16-gauge sterling silver wire a little more than half of the way around your mandrel.

2. Shape it to the desired finger around the largest knuckle and adjust it so the ends point straight up.

3. Trim one end so it extends above the top of your finger by ¾" (1.9cm) and use roundnose pliers to bend it inward into a loop in the same plane as the curve of the ring.

4. Retest for fit. The cut end of the loop should be just above the surface of your finger.

5. Trim the other end as in step 3. Roll it into a matching loop.

6. Open both loops with chain-nose pliers and thread the wrapped loops at each end of the crystal flower onto them. Finally close the loops tightly (photo 14).

Note: To increase the size of the ring slightly, make the loops a little smaller; making them a little larger will decrease the ring size.

STRINGING THE NECKLACE

My necklace fits at the neckline and is 16½" (42cm) long. It has eight flowers with 8mm glass pearls and three with 12mm glass pearls. For a longer necklace, I suggest that you add more glass pearls at the back; the pearl flowers are less likely to flip on a short necklace.

1. String an 11/0 Delica, a crimp bead, and a 10/0 Delica on one end of a 20"-24" (51-61cm) length of flexible beading wire. Thread the tail through the loop on one of the clasp parts and pass it back through the beads and crimp.

Tighten the wire to form a small loop that has some ease and crimp the crimp bead (see Crimping, p. 6). Trim off the short tail with wire cutters.

2. String a small glass pearl, a 15/0, a large glass pearl, and approximately 17 size 11/0 Delicas. Thread the beaded wire through the loops on a small pearl flower, adjusting the 17 Delicas so that 1"-1½" of beads extend past each loop.

3. String a large pearl, 17 Delicas, and another small flower and adjust as before. The pearl flowers should slightly overlap the ends of the large pearl.

4. Repeat step 3, then string another large pearl.

5. String 22-23 Delicas and center a large flower over them.

6. String a large pearl, 17 Delicas and a small flower, a large pearl, 22-23 Delicas and a large flower, a large pearl, 17 Delicas and a small flower, a large pearl, and 22-23 Delicas and the third large flower.

7. Repeat steps 4 through 2 in reverse so the ends match.

8. Tighten the wire so it's snug, but not rigid, and end with an 11/0 Delica, a crimp, and a 10/0.

Thread the tail through the loop on the other clasp part and back through the final 3 beads. Tighten to form a small loop with ease and crimp the crimp.

Trim the wire tail flush.

Spiral Rope
with a Twist

Spiral rope is one of the easiest beading stitches, but it offers as many possible variations as you can imagine.

MATERIALS

All Necklaces:

G-S Hypo Cement
SINGLE STRAND NECKLACE 19" (48cm) total length at center
7-10g Delica beads, size 8/0 (green luster topaz, DBL122)
7-10g Delica beads, size 10/0 (green-lined crystal AB, DBM60)
5g Delica beads, size 11/0 (bronze-lined light olive, DB908)
23-25 Swarovski bicone crystals, 4mm, crystal starlight
70 Freshwater pearls, 4-5mm, light bronze
Beading thread, Miyuki or K-O, green
Beading needles, size 12 or 13
Sterling silver hook-and-eye clasp
    (mine is from PacificSilverworks.com)
2 Sterling silver clamshell bead tips
2 Seed beads, size 15/0, any color
2 Sterling silver split rings, 5mm
2 Sterling silver large-hole beads, 6 x 5mm; hole 3.4mm (RioGrande.com)

Twisted Necklaces

Beading needles, size 10 or 12

GREEN NECKLACE: 17½" (44.5cm) beadwork (at left, p. 30):
15-20g Delica beads, size 8/0 (matte dark olive, DBL311)
15-20g Delica beads, size 10/0 (green-lined crystal AB, DBM60)
10g Delica beads, size 11/0 (transparent chartreuse, DB174)
Beading thread, Miyuki or K-O, green
Large toggle clasp (mine is moss agate with sterling silver
    from KamolBeads@yahoo.com)
6" Sterling silver round wire, 20-gauge, half hard
2 Sterling silver wide-mouth cones, 10mm (PacificSilverworks.com)

BLUE/BRONZE NECKLACE: 21½" (54.5cm) of beadwork:
15-20g Delica beads, size 8/0 (metallic bronze, DBL22)
15-20g Delica beads, size 10/0 (transparent light blue AB, DBM179)
10g Delica beads, size 11/0 (dark blue iris, DB5)
Beading thread, Miyuki or K-O, blue
6" Sterling silver or gold-filled round wire, 20-gauge, half hard
Pewter toggle clasp, antique gold (TierraCast #6064-26)
2 Pewter cones, 11.5 x 8.4mm antique gold (TierraCast #5666-26)
2 Pewter bead caps, 5 x 2.5mm, antique gold (TierraCast #5570-26)

*A Spiral rope consists of two parts: the core
and the outside beads that spiral around the core.
Unless you use very small core beads and much*
*larger beads for the outside, the core beads will
show a little, so your choice of core color is
important. The core beads also need to have
large holes since you sew through each one
four to six times. Size 10/0 Delicas are ideal for
the core.*

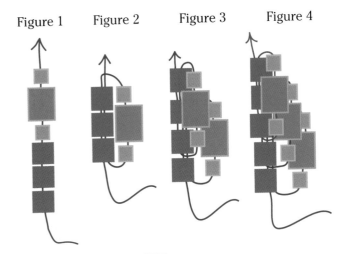

Figure 1   Figure 2   Figure 3   Figure 4

WEAVING A SPIRAL ROPE

Work with single thread as long as is comfortable.
Some size 11/0 Delicas will slide inside 8/0s. Either pick
beads that don't or fill the 8/0 with 2-3 extra 11/0s. When
you position the outer beads, be careful to keep the filler
beads inside the 8/0s.

1. To begin any of the necklaces, string 3 size 10/0 beads
for the core then 1 size 11/0, 1 size 8/0, and 1 size 11/0,
leaving an 8" (20cm) tail (figure 1).

2. Sew through the 3 size 10/0s again toward the first 11/0
and tighten the thread. The 11/0s and 8/0 will be alongside
the 3 core 10/0s (figure 2).

3. Pick up 1 core bead and the 3 outer beads (11/0, 8/0, and
11/0). Skip the bottommost core bead and sew up the top 3
core beads (figure 3).

Be careful always to position the 3 outer beads on the
same side of the previously added outer beads. If you position them to the left as shown in the figures, the spiral will
form in a clockwise direction; if they are to the right, the
spiral will go counterclockwise.

4. Pick up 1 core bead and the 3 outer beads (11/0, 8/0, and
11/0). Sew up the top 3 core beads (figure 4).

5. For the single strand necklace, work 5" (12.7cm) in this manner (62-64 size 8/0 Delicas).

6. Work about 3" (7.6cm) substituting pearls for the size 8/0 Delicas (34-35 pearls).

7. Work about 1¾" substituting 4mm bicone crystals for the pearls (23-24 crystals).

8. Repeat step 6 then step 5, ending with at least an 8" (20cm) thread tail.

9. Begin the twisted necklaces as in steps 1-3 and repeat step 4 until the rope is 8-10" (20-25cm) longer than twice the desired finished length of twisted rope.

The length of the cones and clasp are extra.

But what if you want more than a single strand? No problem! as the green and blue permanently twisted necklaces illustrates.

I've had the massive moss agate toggle clasp that I used for the twisted green spiral rope for almost ten years but have never had the right piece for it until now. I got it from Kamol, a Thai bead trader based in Seattle, but haven't seen any more in recent years, so I decided to repeat this necklace in blue and bronze to show you how lovely it looks with readily available pewter cones and clasp by TierraCast.

If you're going to take the time to make a beautiful piece of bead jewelry, it's important that it also finish beautifully. Findings don't have to cost a fortune to complement your jewelry in terms of color, scale, and style.

My green rope was 44" (1.12m) long before twisting and the blue rope was 53" (1.35m) long.

10. To add thread, sew into the core about 10 beads from the end. Go up 2-3 beads and tie a pair of half hitches (see Knots, p. 6). Repeat 2-3 more times, ending by exiting the same bead as the needle with the short thread.

Work 8-10 repeats; then end the short thread in the new work the same way you secured the new thread.

My idea with this project was to use the same outer and core bead pattern to produce vastly different looking ropes.

The elegant single strand necklace contrasts the green core with a rosy topaz luster size 8/0 main outer bead at the ends, but in the front it substitutes small pearls and 4mm crystals for a thicker, dressier effect.

FINISHING THE SINGLE STRAND NECKLACE

1. String an 11/0 Delica. Then sew into a clamshell bead tip (toward the hook). String a 15/0 bead of any color.

2. Sew out the bottom of the bead tip and through the 11/0 and 3 core beads (photo 1).

3. Tie a pair of half hitches around the thread entering the final outer beads.

4. Sew back up the three core beads and repeat the thread path in steps 1-2, going down 4 core beads before knotting. If possible, reinforce the connection to the bead tip once more. Dot the thread and 15/0 inside the bead tip with a drop of G-S Hypo Cement.

5. End the thread by sewing down a few core beads and tying a pair of half hitches. Continue down the core, knotting at least twice more. End by going through a few more core beads before trimming the thread.

6. Attach a split ring to the loop on one of the clasp parts. Then thread the large-hole bead over the open bead tip and push it down to reveal the bead

tip's handle. Use roundnose pliers to curl the handle around the split ring so that the tip of the hook meets its base a tiny bit lower than the top of the clamshell (photo 2).

7. Put 2-3 drops of Hypo Cement inside the bead tip. Then use the tip of your chain-nose pliers to press the clamshell closed inside the large-hole bead (photo 3). Be careful not to mark the large-hole bead. Hint: Wrap the pliers jaws with masking tape. Hold the clamshell closed with your pliers for a minute or two until the glue has begun to set.

8. Repeat steps 1-7 with the starting thread tail and the other clasp part.

FINISHING THE
TWISTED NECKLACES

1. Cut a 12" (30cm) piece of beading thread and have it ready.

2. Secure the last few beads at one end of the rope to a stationary object. (If you only secure the thread tail, it will break when you twist the strand.)

3. Straighten the rope and holding the last few beads at the other end, twist it in one direction until it lumps back onto itself. You want a lot of lumping for a tightly twisted rope and less for a softly twisted rope.

4. Grasp the strand at about the center and bring the free thread tail up to the bound one with the ends of the beadwork even.

5. Massage the doubled rope to distribute the twist evenly, allowing the two halves of the rope to twist around each other.

If you like the look, continue with the next step.

If the twist is too loose or too tight, separate the ends and continue twisting the free end or release some of the twist. Reunite the ends and even the twist.

6. Tie the two thread tails together against the beads with a surgeon's knot to contain the twist.

Then center the thread from step 1 at the fold and tie it tightly around the rope, so both ends have a pair of 5"- 6" (12.7-15cm) thread tails.

7. Cut two 3" (7.6cm) pieces of 20-gauge sterling or gold-filled wire and make a small single-wrapped loop at one end of each piece.

8. Thread each of the tails at one end of the rope through a loop from opposite directions and tie them tightly to the loop.

Repeat several times, ending by tying the threads to the wire above the wrap. Repeat with the other loop and pair of threads.

Secure the knots with G-S Hypo Cement and let it dry completely (photo 4).

9. Thread one of the wires into a cone from the wide end and pull the beadwork up inside the cone.

If any of the loop or knot shows, flatten the loop and bend it up against the wire (photo 5). (This problem will occur if the loop is too large or the cones are a bit short and/or narrow.)

10. Thread the wire into the cone again and string a bead against the top of the cone to conceal its hole. (I used a 10/0 on the green necklace and a tiny bead cap on the blue one.)

11. Leaving room for 2-3 wraps, start a medium to large wrapped loop and thread the loop of a clasp part into it.

Wrap the wire tail around the wire exiting the cone until the wraps push the cone down against the rope as tightly as possible (photo 6).

12. Repeat steps 9-11 with the other wire, cone, and clasp part.

Sparkling Herringbone Bracelets

I love the fluidity and drape of Ndebele Herringbone, but perhaps even more I love the easy way it can be embellished by floating beads between stitches. If the float beads become gradually larger, the herringbone band becomes wider, which looks complicated but isn't.

The only problem with this technique is that the float beads are a row below the row on which you add them. That means that at one end of the band the floating beads are close to the

end, but on the other, they aren't.

Since I'm a perfectionist, that bothered me so I figured out a way to rework the beginning and final ends to make them match. It's a bit complicated, so if you're not a perfectionist, don't worry about that part of this project. With all the sparkle from the Swarovski crystals, no one will notice anyway.

These bracelets are beautiful... you'll probably want to make one in every color of the rainbow.

Brick Stitch
see page 9

Ndebele Herringbone
see pages 8 - 9

MATERIALS

Note: 4 rows add ½" (1.3cm)

GOLDEN BRACELET 6" - 7½" (15-19cm):

10-12g Delica beads, size 8/0 (transparent light topaz, DBL121)

7-10g Delica beads, size 10/0 (dark topaz AB, DBM170)

7g Delica beads, size 11/0 (transparent golden topaz AB, DB100)

5-7g Miyuki seed beads, size 11/0 (dark topaz, rose luster AB, 257)

3-5g Miyuki seed beads, size 15/0 (honey topaz, 887)

22-34 Swarovski bicone crystals, 3mm, topaz

60-84 Swarovski bicone crystals, 3mm, golden shadow

14 Swarovski bicone crystals, 4mm, topaz

44 Swarovski bicone crystals, 4mm, crystal chili pepper

4-5 Swarovski bicone crystals, 6mm, topaz

Beading thread, Miyuki or K-O size B, gold or Fireline

Beading needles, size 12

Sterling silver 5-loop slide clasp

ROSE BRACELET 6½" - 8" (16.5-20cm):

10-12g Delica beads, size 8/0 (sparkle peony pink-lined crystal, DBL902)

7-10g Delica beads, size 10/0 (rose gold luster cuts, DBM103C)

7g Delica beads, size 11/0 (silver-lined pink semi-matte, DB624)

5-7g Miyuki seed beads, size 11/0 (pink-lined crystal, 272)

3-5g Miyuki seed beads, size 15/0 (sparkle peony pink-lined crystal, 1524)

22-34 Swarovski bicone crystals, 3mm, light rose

52-76 Swarovski bicone crystals, 3mm, rose

16 Swarovski bicone crystals, 4mm, light rose ice

42 Swarovski bicone crystals, 4mm, topaz AB 2X

3 Swarovski bicone crystals, 6mm, fuchsia

Beading thread, Miyuki or K-O size B, pink or Fireline

Beading needles, size 12

Silver-tone dressmaker's skirt/pants hook

Figure 1

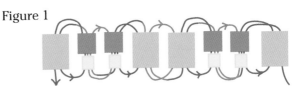

HOW-TO

Use doubled thread to make these bracelets. Lengthen or shorten them in the 3mm crystal sections at the beginning and end, adding or omitting 2 rows per end for every half inch (1.3cm).

If you wish to make the ends match, be extremely careful not to split the thread in the ladder start and the first two rows.

1. In this herringbone pattern a stacked 10/0 and 11/0 equals one 8/0. In order to be going the right direction for the first herringbone row, start the bracelet with a brick stitch ladder of 8 stitches, patterning it upside down as follows (figure 1):

Leave a 16" (41cm) thread tail.

Figure 2

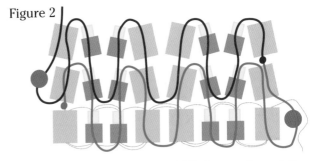

a. Pick up an 8/0, a 10/0, and an 11/0. Sew up through the 8/0 again in the original direction, pulling the two smaller beads next to it. Sew down the two smaller beads.

b. Pick up an 11/0 and a 10/0. Sew down the first pair of small beads and up the second.

c. Pick up an 8/0 and sew up the second pair of small beads then down the 8/0.

d. Pick up another 8/0 and sew down the previous one then up the new one.

e. Pick up a 10/0 and an 11/0 and sew up the last 8/0 then down the pair of small beads.

f. Repeat steps b and c. Then turn the ladder over so the needle is coming up the end 8/0 (figure 2, bottom left, light blue dot). Notice that the 11/0s are now above the 10/0s in each pair.

2. Work 2 herringbone rows of 4 stitches in the color pattern.

a. Pick up an 8/0, an 11/0, and a 10/0 and sew down the first small bead pair from the end on the ladder. Do Not split the thread (figure 2, blue line).

b. Sew up the second small bead pair and pick up a 10/0, an 11/0, and an 8/0. Sew down the first middle 8/0 and up the second.

c. Repeat step a then b.

d. To turn at the end of the row and position your needle to begin the next row, pick up an 11/0 seed bead and sew up the last 8/0 added (figure 2, right, blue line to dark blue dot).

e. Repeat steps a-d for the second row (figure 2, dark blue line).

3. For the first crystal section, work as follows:

a. Work the first stitch, an 8/0 and a bead pair. With the needle coming down the stack below, pick up a 3mm shadow crystal (topaz bracelet) or a 3mm rose crystal (rose bracelet). Then sew up the adjacent stack (figure 3, green dot and line).

b. Pick up the beads for the second stitch and sew down the first middle 8/0. Pick up a 3mm topaz (topaz bracelet) or a 3mm light rose crystal (rose bracelet) and sew up the other middle 8/0.

c. Add the beads for the third stitch and sew down the first of the pair of stacks, repeating the crystal pattern in step a.

d. Coming up the second stack, pick up the beads for the fourth stitch and sew down the end 8/0. Turn with an 11/0 seed (figure 3, green to light green line on right).

4. Work a total of 11 3mm crystal rows for either bracelet (figure 3, light green line shows second crystal row). Remember to add or omit half the number of rows you need to lengthen or shorten your bracelet in this section. These directions make a 6" topaz bracelet and a 6½" rose bracelet.

5. If you want the end and the beginning to look the same, work this step; if not, omit it:

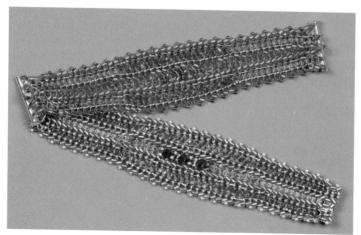

After you've worked 4-5 rows with crystals, pick out the ladder thread. All the ladder beads except the last one remain attached to the first herringbone row. String a temporary stop bead to hold the end 8/0 in place.

6. Work 2 rows with 3mm crystals between the outer stitches and a 15/0, 4mm topaz (rose) crystal, and a 15/0 between the center stitches.

Figure 3

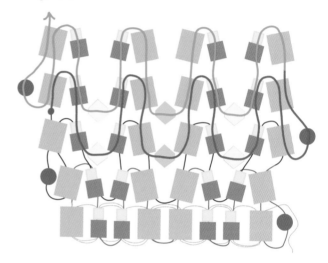

Note: Always string a 15/0 on each side of the 4 and 6mm crystals to protect the thread. They will not be mentioned in future.

7. Work 6 rows with 4mm chili pepper (topaz AB 2X) crystals between the outer stitches and 4mm topaz (rose) crystals between the center stitches.

8. For the center section, continue using the same 4mm crystals between the outer stitches. Work the following pattern between the center stitches:

a. First and third rows: 10/0, 15/0 seed, 11/0 seed, 15/0 seed, 10/0 (topaz bracelet); or 10/0, 11/0 seed, 10/0, 11/0 seed, 10/0 (rose bracelet).

b. Second row: 15/0 seed, 6mm crystal, 15/0 seed.

Make 2 3-row repeats on the topaz bracelet and 3 on the rose bracelet (each repeat adds ⅜" (1cm).

9. Repeat steps 7, 6, and 4 after the center section.

10. After the last row on which you add crystals, work 1 herringbone row with just beads.

11. If you are not worrying about making the ends look identical, join the beads of the last row to simulate a

ladder as shown in figure 2 of "Glorious Beaded Bead Bracelet."

12. To add and end thread, work the first 2 stitches of a row. Thread a new needle, and beginning about 10 rows below the last stitch worked, sew up the beads in the first stack of the last stitch worked, tying pairs of half hitches around the thread every few beads at least 3 times (see Knots, p. 6).

When you get to the top, repeat the thread path of the last new stitch and resume beading with the new thread. End the short thread the same way you anchored the new thread by sewing and knotting down the second stack of the last stitch worked.

Figure 4

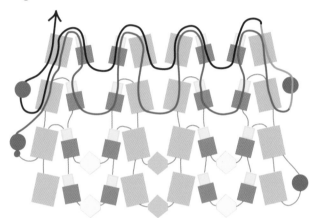

MAKING THE ENDS LOOK ALIKE (OPTIONAL)

Because the ends overlap on the rose bracelet, I worked the 3-row version on the final end and attached the hook part of the clasp. The starting end has 4 rows beyond the crystals since its first row is hidden. The slide clasp on the topaz bracelet necessitated 3- or 4-row versions on both ends.

FINAL END

1. After working the last crystal row, pick up a turn bead and work 1 more row with just beads (figure 4 blue dot and line). There will be 3 rows above the last crystals; if you want 4 rows, work 2 plain rows in this step.
2. At the end of the last row, pick up a turn bead and come out the last 8/0 added (figure 4, green line).
3. To join the beads of the last row in a herringbone pattern, go down the first pair and up the second, down the first center 8/0 and up the second, then down the adjacent pair and up the last pair (figure 4, dark blue line).

End the row by going down the last 8/0 and the one below it. Add a turn bead and come back out the last 8/0. You are now ready to attach the clasp at this end.

Figure 5

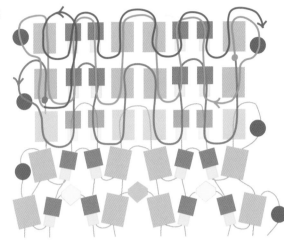

STARTING END

1. To finish the starting end, you already unpicked the ladder (tinted lighter in figure 5). Remove the stop bead. If you didn't split a thread, you have enough with the long starting tail to work the end rows. Otherwise, end the short starting tail and begin a new doubled thread so that it exits the last 8/0 of the ladder pointing away from the bracelet.

This method leaves you with 4 rows below the first crystals.

2. For the first row, pick up an 8/0 and an 11/0 seed/turn bead (figure 5, purple dot and line at left):
a. Sew into the first ladder bead toward the bracelet.
b. Sew out the first 11/0, 10/0 pair on the ladder and *pick up an 11/0, 2 10/0s, and an 11/0. Sew into the next ladder pair then out the adjacent 8/0.
c. Pick up 2 8/0s and sew into the second center ladder 8/0 then out the adjacent pair. Repeat step b from *.
d. End the row by picking up an 8/0 (figure 5, purple line to green dot).
3. Begin the second and last row (figure 5, green line) by picking up another 8/0 and a turn bead.
a. Sew into the 8/0 you picked up in step d above then out the adjacent pair.
b. Pick up an 11/0, 2 10/0s, and an 11/0 and sew into the next pair of row 1 then out the first center 8/0.
c. Pick up 2 8/0s and sew into the second center 8/0 then out the next pair. Repeat step b. End by coming out the end 8/0.

end 8/0 on row 2 (figure 5, blue line). Come back out the first pair of row 2 and go down the second pair.

b. Come out the first middle 8/0 and go down the second.

c. Come out the next pair and go down the last pair.

d. End by coming out the end 8/0. Follow the green thread path (figure 5 at right) through the turn bead and down the end column to end the thread securely.

Figure 6

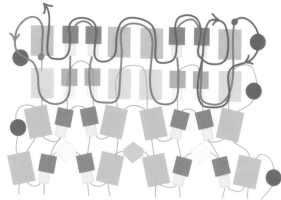

5. For a 3-row ending, end step 2 with an 8/0 and a turn bead (figure 6, purple line to blue dot at right). Sew back into the end ladder bead and work step 4 on the only added row (figure 6, blue line).

Figure 7

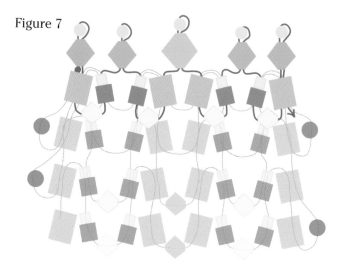

ATTACHING A SLIDE CLASP
CRYSTAL FRINGE

1. Before attaching each clasp part, finish the end with a crystal fringe to conceal the clasp.

   With your needle exiting an end 8/0, pick up a 4mm chili pepper crystal and a 15/0. Sew back down the crystal and the 8/0 with the needle coming out the front of the bracelet.

2. Pick up a 3mm golden shadow crystal and sew out the first pair. Pick up a chili pepper and a 15/0 and sew down the crystal and into the adjacent pair.

3. Pick up a 3mm golden shadow crystal and sew out the first center 8/0. Pick up a 6mm topaz crystal and a 15/0 and go back down the crystal and into the other center 8/0.

4. Repeat step 2.

5. Pick up a 3mm golden shadow crystal and sew out the last 8/0, pick up a 4mm chili pepper crystal and a 15/0, and sew back down the crystal and the 8/0 with the needle coming out the back side of the bracelet (figure 7).

Figure 8

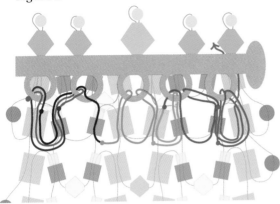

CLASP ATTACHMENT

1. With the needle exiting the bottom of the end 8/0 on the back (figure 8, blue dot at left), go through the first clasp loop then down the second 8/0 from the end. You will attach the clasp loops to the beads of the second row from the end.

2. Sew up the adjacent pair and go through the second clasp loop (figure 8, red line). Sew down the pair then up the 8/0 in step 1. Go through the first clasp loop (figure 8, maroon line).

3. Sew back down the 8/0 then up the adjacent pair. Go through the second loop then down the next pair (figure 8, dark burgundy line).

4. Come up the first center 8/0 and go through the third clasp loop then back down the same 8/0. Come up the next 8/0, go through the third loop and down the same 8/0 (figure 8, orange line).

5. Come up the next pair and go through the fourth clasp loop. Then go down the pair and up the adjacent center 8/0 (figure 8, light green line).

6. Go through the fourth loop and down the same pair. Come up last pair and go through the fourth clasp loop (figure 8, dark green line).

7. Go and down the same pair then up the last 8/0. Sew through the fifth clasp loop then go down the same 8/0 (figure 8, purple line).

8. Go up the last pair again and through the fifth loop. Come down the pair and up the end 8/0 on the next to last row. Continue through the top 8/0 and come out on the front of the bracelet between the first pair of fringe crystals (figure 8, magenta line).

FINISH THE FRONT

1. To finish concealing the clasp on the front, pick up a golden shadow crystal and sew down the end pair to the back and through the second loop (Note: In figure 9, the only beads sewn through have a colored line through them; otherwise you sew behind beads). Go through end loop toward the front (figure 9, magenta to purple line at right).

2. Sew through the new golden shadow then to the back through the second loop. Come through the third loop to the front (figure 9, purple to green line). Pick up a golden shadow and position it between the first center 8/0 and the second pair from the edge. Then sew to the back and through the second loop (figure 9, green line).

3. Come to the front through the third loop and go behind the second center 8/0 to the top. Pick up a golden shadow and sew to the back and through the fourth loop behind the first pair (figure 9, blue line).

Figure 9

4. Working on the back, sew through the third loop to the front and down the next to the end 8/0 after the center. Come up the next pair and through the fourth loop to the back. Go through the fifth loop to the front (figure 9, burgundy line).

5. Between the edge top 8/0 and the adjacent pair, pick up a final golden shadow (photo 2). Sew to the back and through the fourth loop (figure 9, red line). End the thread in the beadwork.

6. Close the clasp to begin attaching the second part. Open it as soon as you've gone through the first loop.

2

Petal Earrings

I love to wear earrings. When I make a pair, I want it to be special. Not content with a flat piece of triangular brick stitch, I began experimenting with ways to give earrings depth and texture.

The result is these softly curled petals that turn a geometric shape into an organic, abstract flower.

Peyote Stitch see page 7
Brick Stitch see page 9

MATERIALS
Petal Earrings
5g Delica beads, size 10/0 (cream-lined crystal AB, DBM52)
5g Delica beads, size 11/0 (transparent light topaz, DB101)
5g Delica beads, size 11/0 (gold-lined milky white, DB230)
3g Miyuki seed beads, size 15/0 (transparent light topaz, 2439)
3g Miyuki seed beads, size 15/0 (ochre-lined light topaz, 2238)
6 Swarovski bicone crystals, 4mm, ruby
2 Freshwater potato pearls, approx. 6.4 x 7.4mm, white
Beading thread, Miyuki or K-O size B or Nymo B, gold
Beading needles, size 12 or 13
2"- 3" (5-7.6cm) Gold-filled round wire, 22-gauge, half hard
2 Post earring clutches
Beading pliers and small metal file

HOW-TO
You first construct a brick stitch triangular base, then use a variation of 3-bead edging stitch to make a bridge for the top triangles on each side of the base triangle.

The top triangles are woven in peyote stitch then edged.

Finally you join them in the center and fill the opening with a bead-ringed pearl.

Figure 1

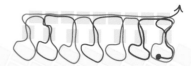

EARRINGS
BASE
TRIANGLE:
For each earring, use 10/0 Delicas to brick stitch a triangle with a 12-bead ladder base and a single bead at the top (see p. 9).

SIDE TRIANGLES:
1. Begin the transparent topaz size 11/0 Delica side triangle with a bridge similar to 3-bead edging. Anchor the thread in the 10/0 base triangle and exit the edge bead on row 3, sewing toward the ladder (figure 1, red dot).
2. Pick up 4 beads and sew through the row 4 edge bead toward row 3. Then sew through the fourth bead toward the third and tighten the thread and pull it into a vertical position (figure 1, red dot and line).

3. For the second bridge stitch, pick up 2 beads. Go through the next edge bead toward the previous one (through row 5 toward row 4) and sew up the second bead strung.

4. Pick up 3 beads for the third stitch and sew through the next edge bead toward the previous one. Sew up the last new bead.

5. Finish with a 2-bead, a 3-bead, and a 2-bead stitch (figure 1 red line). As you work, push the bridge up perpendicular to the brick stitch triangle.

6. After sewing up the last bead strung continue back to the start through the 9 horizontal beads. Sew down the first bridge bead and through the row 3 edge bead toward row 4 (figure 2, light blue line). Sew back up the first vertical bead and out the first horizontal bead toward the starting edge, centering it over the first vertical bead (figure 1, blue line).

Figure 2

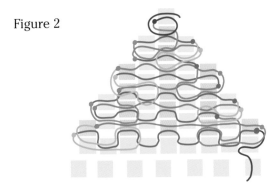

7. Work a row of peyote (see p. 7) on the horizontal beads, placing 5 beads over the odd-numbered beads (figure 2, blue line). Make a hard turn (figure 2, orange line) and work a 4-bead row back to the start (figure 2, light blue line).

8. Work an 11-row triangle as shown in figure 2 with each stair-stepped edge 2 beads tall. The turns at the end of the rows will vary as shown in figure 2. (Odd-numbered rows are shown with darker beads and dark blue lines and even-numbered rows have lighter beads and light blue lines.

Yellow and purple lines indicate the complex turns.

The color of each dot indicates the beginning of that colored line.)

Square stitch a final bead to the row 11 bead as shown at the top of figure 2 (dark blue line) and work the thread to the middle of the triangle to end it.

Note: If you want to make the second earring a mirror image of the first, hold the bases with the ladders to the outside and start the transparent triangle on the same side (top or bottom).

Figure 3

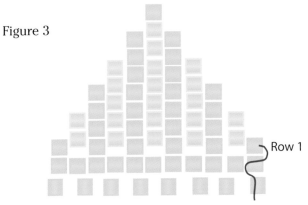

Row 1

9. Use gold-lined 11/0s for the other two triangles. Start the bridge for the second side triangle on row 3 and end in the 3-bead row. There will be 11 top bridge beads, a triangle with 14 peyote rows and a final square stitched bead.

Work hard and easy turns as needed just as you did on the first side triangle. Beads of odd-numbered rows are shown in the darker color (figure 3).

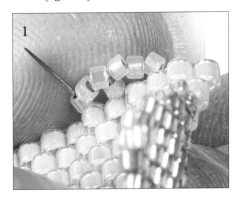

Figure 4

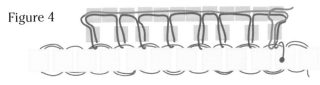

10. Starting the bridge for the triangle that comes from the ladder edge is a bit trickier because you are connecting the bridge beads to thread loops rather than beads.

You must vary the number of beads you pick up for each stitch to produce a flat, straight base as you sew under each thread loop. You may need to use your best judgment despite the specificity of these directions.

11. Weave in the thread to exit the second ladder bead and sew under the second thread loop from the end (figure 4, red line).

12. Pick up 4 gold-lined 11/0s and sew under the next loop. Sew up the last bead. Following figure 4, pick up 3 and go under the next loop and back up the last bead (photo 1 shows this step on the earring).

Pick up 2, 3, 3, 2, and 3 (photo 1), sewing under the third loop from the ladder end for the last stitch (figure 4, blue line).

13. Come back up the last bead and sew through the 12 horizontal beads between the vertical beads (figure 4, orange line).

Sew down the first bead, through the starting thread loop, back up the first bead and through the second toward the start, centering it over the vertical bead (figure 4, purple line).

Figure 5

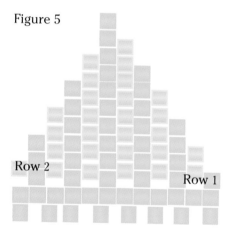

Row 2

Row 1

14. Figure 5 shows the pattern for this peyote stitch triangle, which has 17 rows and ends with a bead square stitched to the last peyote bead.

Beads on the odd-numbered rows are darker than those on the even-numbered rows.

Figure 6

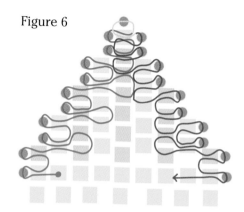

FINISHING THE TRIANGLES:

For the edging on the 11/0 triangles, use ochre-lined 15/0s on the transparent topaz triangle and transparent topaz 15/0s on the gold-lined triangles.

1. Start at one end of the horizontal bridge row, come out the edge bead, pick up a 15/0, and sew back into the bead (figure 6, blue dot and line at left). On the second row of vertical pairs, you'll be able to just sew out the next edge bead, but on shorter or longer rows, you'll have to go in another bead half a step above or below the edge bead you've just edged to be able to come out the adjacent bead, then the next edge bead (figure 6).

2. Edge on each side of the single-bead rows and sew a third bead above the tip bead (figure 6, light blue line).

Note: You may need to use a size 13 needle to edge the beads at the tip because they have a lot of thread inside.

3. Then edge down the other side of the triangle (figure 6, purple line on right).

End the thread in the triangle.

POST FOR EARRINGS

1. Cut a 1" (2.5cm) piece of 22-gauge gold-filled wire.

Insert the end through the 10/0 brick triangle from the back to the front and go through the fourth bead from the transparent petal edge in the fourth row from the ladder.

2. Make sure the end that goes through the bead on the front, is flat, and extends beyond it slightly.

Bend the long end on the back at a right angle to the brick stitch triangle (photo 2).

3. Secure the wire bend on the front by sewing over it back and forth through the beads on each side (photo 3).

Trim the post to the desired length and file the end smooth and round. Lightly groove the post about 1/8" (3mm) from the end with wire cutters.

3. Continue through the first 3 beads of the first spoke.

Then sew through the middle bead on each of the 3 spokes and pull them tightly together to make a platform for the pearl (photo 6).

4. Use size 15/0 transparent topaz beads for the center decoration.

Coming out a center of the platform, string 2 size 15/0s, the pearl, and 2 more 15/0s. Sew into a center bead on the far side of the platform (photo 7).

5. Sew up the 2 beads on the first side of the pearl and string 3-6 beads to reach the nearest spoke.

Go through the spoke bead closest

to the pearl's side. Then go through the last bead of the 3-6 away from the group. Repeat around to encircle the pearl (photo 8). End by sewing through a spoke bead then the top bead next to the pearl's hole. Sew through all the beads in the circle around the pearl once or twice.

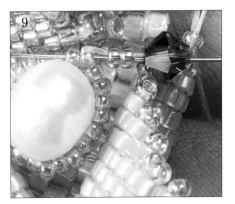

6. Bring the needle out a ring bead centered between two petals. String 2 15/0s, a 4mm crystal, and a 15/0. Go back through the crystal and the 2 15/0s then the ring bead you exited in the same direction (photo 9). Sew around the ring to the next space between petals and repeat twice more.

7. Sew through the ring once more if possible, tying off with pairs of half hitches between ring beads 2-3 times.

EMBELLISHING THE CENTER

1. Begin a thread in one of the peyote triangles so that it comes out the center bead about 3 rows up from the bridge row (photo 4).

2. String 5 transparent topaz 11/0s and go into the matching bead on the next triangle. Repeat around (photo 5).

Floral
Stick Pin &
Earrings

*Combine peyote stitch
and tubular herringbone
and flat herringbone.*

Peyote Stitch
see page 7
Herringbone Stitch
see pages 8 - 9

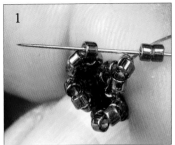

Figure 1

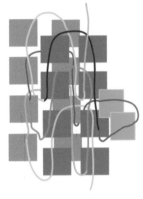

I enjoy creating flowers that have a realistic look. For this pin and earrings, I've used peyote stitch to make the five petals of the flower, tubular herringbone for the branching stems, and flat herringbone for the leaves.

My variations on these classic stitches make this project a bit more complicated than most of the other projects included here.

MATERIALS
5-7g Size 10/0 Delicas, crimson DBM105
3-5g Size 10/0 hex-cut Delicas, rose luster DBM103C
10g Size 11/0 Delicas, trans. green luster DB175
2g Size 11/0 Delicas, trans. yellow luster DB171
Beading thread, Miyuki or K-O pink, red, and green
Beading needles, size 12 and 13
6-8 in. (15-20cm) Sterling silver round wire, half-hard,
    18-gauge for pin
Purchased earwires OR use 6 in. (15cm) of Sterling silver
    round wire, half-hard, 20-gauge for earwires
Needle file to sharpen pin and smooth earwires

HOW TO
STICK PIN
    Main stem and sepal

1. Using green beads and thread, make a herringbone tube that has four stitches. Do not begin with a ladder. Use the directions for making a herringbone start, p. 8.

2. Work a total of 9 rounds. On the tenth round, pick up 2 beads between any two stitches on the tube (photo 1 and figure 1, red line). (Note: Figure 1 shows only a 2-stitch tube for clarity.)
    You'll use these beads later to begin the stem for the bud. Ignore them now.

3. Continue weaving the 4-stitch tube until you have 24 rounds.

4. On round 25, begin two increase stitches (see "Herringbone" figure 4, p. 9), work the first stitch. Then begin an increase by picking up 1 bead. Work stitches #2 and 3 normally. Begin the second increase before the fourth stitch by picking up 1 bead.

5. Work the fourth stitch and step up to begin round 26. After the first stitch, pick up 2 beads. Then work the second and third stitches. Pick up 2 beads, work the fourth stitch, and step up.

6. Work 6 stitches around until the stem is 30 rows long.

7. Form the sepal on round 31 by picking up 3 beads for the first stitch. Sew down 2 beads then up 2 beads to begin the next stitch (photo 2). Repeat around, then end the thread securely with a couple of pairs of half hitches. Leave the thread, which should be 8-12 in. (20-30cm) long, in place.

BUD STEM

1. Secure a new thread that's about 54-in. long (1.4m) into the stem and exit round 10 next to the 2 beads you added in step 2, sewing up through the bead before them.

2. Pick up 2 beads and sew down the next bead on round 10. Then sew back up the bead you exited in step 1 (photo 3 and figure 2, orange lines).

3. Sew up the first new bead (light orange to wheat line). Pick up 2 and sew down the second new bead. Then sew up the adjacent bead of the pair you added on round 10. Pick up 2 and go down the other added bead (wheat to burgundy lines).

4. Step up through the first bead from step 2 and the new bead above it (burgundy line at left). Pick up 2 and go down the second new bead. Then sew up the first new bead of the other new stitch. Pick up 2 and sew down the second bead of the stitch. Continue through 2 beads of the first stitch to step up (photo 4).

5. Work this 2-stitch tube for 6 rounds. On the seventh round, string 2 beads between the 2 stitches to serve as the base for the leaf stem.

6. Continue working the 2-stitch tube (ignore the 2 beads added on round 7) until it has 10 rounds.

7. On round 11 begin increasing as in step 4-5 of the main stem to add 2 stitches, one on each side of the round. When you have the 8 beads for the 4 stitches, work 1 round (photo 5).

8. Work a short sepal on the next round by picking up 3 beads for each stitch, but only sew down 1 bead and up 1 bead (photo 6).

9. End the thread with a couple of pairs of half hitches. Then sew the long thread that remains down the stem to come out next to the 2 beads you added on round 7.

10. Begin the 2-stitch, tubular leaf stem by repeating steps 1-4. When you have completed 10 rounds, begin the leaf.

Figure 2

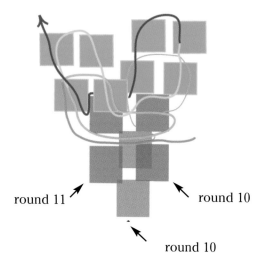

round 11 ↗   ↖ round 10

↖

round 10

LEAF

1. To begin a leaf, spread the two stitches of the stem so they are side by side (figure 3, the light green dot & line shows the thread path of the last stem row). Repeat the thread path with the stitches spread (green dot & line).

2. When you go down the fourth bead, you must work a turn to exit this bead so you can begin the next row. Continue down the bead below then go up the bead next to it (wheat line and dotted line). Then step over and exit the edge bead (see also figure 4, to light orange dot).

3. On row 1, add the 2 beads of the first stitch (light orange line). Pick up an increase bead and come up the first bead of the second stitch. Pick up 2 beads and sew down the second bead of the stitch below (light green beads). Add a stitch at the end of the row by picking up 5 beads and arranging them so 2 beads stack next to the last stitch and 3 beads stack along the outer edge. Sew down through the edge bead on the stem immediately below the spread row (light orange line).

    Then sew back up the 3 outside beads (burgundy line).

Note: The rows begin on the side with the row number.

4. Begin row 2 (burgundy line) by working the first 2 stitches.

    Sew through the increase bead and up the first bead of the third stitch to work the third stitch. Turn and come up the outside bead of the new row (burgundy to wheat line).

5. On row 3, pick up 1 increase bead after the first stitch and again after the second stitch. Turn after the third stitch (wheat to light orange line).

6. Work row 4 like row 3 (light orange to burgundy line).

7. On row 5, pick up 1 increase bead after the first stitch and 2 after the second stitch. Turn (burgundy to wheat line).

8. Row 6 has 4 stitches; do not add an increase bead before the last stitch – just skip the one on row 5 when you come to it. Turn. (wheat to orange line).

9. Work rows 7 (orange), 8 (burgundy), and 9 (wheat) with 4 stitches.

10. On row 10 (orange), work the first three stitches normally. For the last stitch, pick up 3 beads to bring it to a point and end it. Turn by sewing down the bead below the edge bead and up the bead next to it. Continue up the edge bead of the third stitch (orange to burgundy line).

11. Work row 11 with three stitches and turn (burgundy to wheat line).

12.Begin row 12 by picking up 3 beads to point and end the first stitch. Then work the next 2 stitches normally (wheat to orange line).

13. Work rows 13-15 on 2 stitches (orange, burgundy, and wheat lines. To turn at the end of row 15, sew down the bead below the last bead added. Then sew up the bead next to it and the next-to-last bead added (wheat to orange line).

14. Pick up 3 beads and sew down the other middle bead (orange line). Circle back through the beads below the new stitch and the 3 new beads (burgundy line). Then sew down the column to end the thread with 2-3 pairs of half hitches between beads.

    Note to shorten the leaf for the earrings, omit a row in the row 6-9 group and the row 13-15 group.

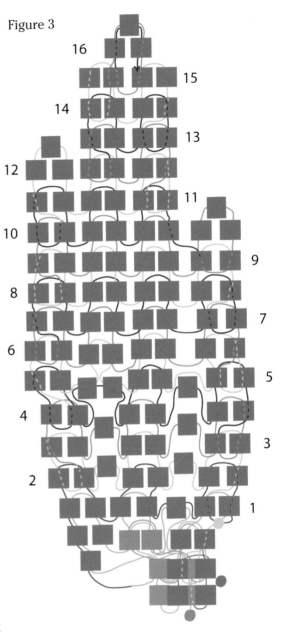

Figure 3

Figure 4

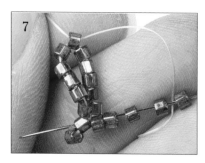

Figure 5

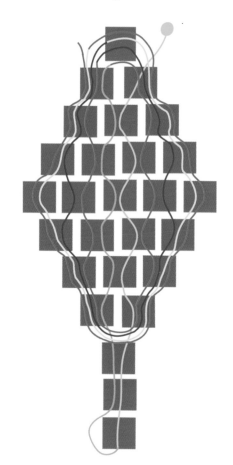

BUD

1. Using pink thread, string 8 pink beads. Leave a 6-8-in. (15-20cm) thread tail. Skip the last bead strung and sew through the seventh toward the first. String 5, go through the first bead away from the tail.

2. String 5 and sew through the last 2 beads strung in step 1 (photo 7). Sew back down the seventh bead.

3. String 5 on the other side of the long loop and go through the bottom bead.

4. Continue adding loops of 5-6 beads between the top two beads and the bottom bead until you can't get through the seventh bead anymore.

5. End with the thread going through the bottom center bead. Tie the thread tails together at the base with a surgeon's knot. Dot the knot with glue and bury the starting tail in a few beads.

6. Pass the thread down into the bud sepal and partway down the stem. Then sew the sepal to the bud in several places to secure it (photo 8). End the pink thread.

FLOWER

Make 5 peyote stitch flower petals as shown in figure 5, using red thread.

1. To begin, string 10 red beads (wheat dot and line).

2. Skip the last bead and sew back through the next 2 toward the start (light blue line at bottom). Pick up a bead, skip the next bead on the strand and go through the next. Add 4 beads in peyote stitch. The last bead will line up against the first bead strung (light blue line).

3. To anchor the last bead, sew down the first bead toward the stem. Peyote stitch 3 beads down toward the stem, ending by going through the seventh bead of the original strand (medium blue line).

4. Turn and sew up the first peyote stitch bead. Add 3 beads in peyote stitch to reach the top (medium blue line on left).

5. Pick up 1 bead and sew down the first bead strung and the first bead added on the right-hand 3-bead row (dark blue line).

6. Add 2 beads in peyote stitch. Then sew diagonally down the last 2 petal beads.

7. Sew diagonally up the bottom 2 petal beads on the left side and add 2 beads in peyote stitch. Sew diagonally up 2 beads and through the single bead at the top (dark blue to yellow line).

8. Sew diagonally down 3 beads on the right, add 1 bead in peyote stitch and go diagonally down the bottom 3 beads. Sew diagonally up the bottom 3 beads on the left, add 1 peyote bead, and go diagonally up the top 3 beads (yellow line).

9. Being careful not to split a thread, sew through all the beads along the outer edge of the petal (blue-green line) and pull the thread to cup the petal.

10. End the thread securely in the petal with a couple of pairs of half hitches. Then end the starting thread in the petal, too.

11. To join the petals, weave a new red thread into one of the petals or use a long thread left on one petal.

12. Bring the thread through the 2 stem beads toward the end. Sew through the 2 stem beads of petal #2 toward the petal. Then sew back down the 2 stem beads of petal #1 (photo 9).

13. Repeat the thread path but only come back down the first bead of petal #1 (photo 10 at left). Sew up the top stem bead of petal #2. End by sewing down both stem beads of petal #1.

14. Sew each petal to the group the same way. Then join the petals on each end.

15. Next ladder stitch the bottom peyote beads of the petals to each other (photo 11).

16. Finally sew down a stem and through the 5 turn beads at the end of the petal stems.

STAMEN

1. Sew the red thread up the inside of the flower stem. String 6 yellow beads, skip the last 3, and sew down the first 3. Pull the fringe tight and set it in the center of the flower opening. Sew back down the flower stem and secure the thread to the end.

2. Sew back through the stem and string 7 beads. Skip the last 3 and sew back through the first 4. Go back down the stem and secure the longer stamen to a bead at the bottom.

3. Make 3 more 7-bead stamens around the shorter center stamen (see the stamens in photo 13).

4. End the red thread in the stem.

5. Insert the flower into the six-stitch sepal and thread a needle on the green thread you left on the sepal. Sew the flower stem into the sepal and attach each sepal point to the base of the flower (photo 12). Then end the thread.

ASSEMBLING THE PIN

1. Experiment with placement of the bud, leaf, and flower and secure them to each other as desired with green thread (photo 13).

2. Cut a 6-8-in. (15-20cm) piece of 18-gauge sterling silver wire and form one end into a slightly open coil that will fit inside the top of the main stem. Use the file to sharpen the other end to a point.

3. Insert the pointed end through the back side of the stem between two stitches from inside to outside about 6-8 rows from the end (photo 14).

4. Use the starting thread tail to sew through the stem and silver coil inside to keep the pin from turning. Then end the thread.

5. Bend the pin down right above where it exits the stem with round-nose pliers (photo 15).

6. Add a new 1-2 yd. (.9-1.8m) green thread to exit one of the end stitches on the stem. Work 2 stitches in flat herringbone for 2 rows. Then join them into a 2-stitch tube by sewing up the first pair of beads (photo 16).

7. Work the tube for 6-8 rows then end it with a leaf.

8. Repeat steps 6-7 with the other two main stem stitches, making this stem a few rows longer than the first.

9. Finally arrange the new leaves and secure them to the other beadwork (photo 17).